Gender, Faith, and Development

Praise for this book

'The timely, thought-provoking essays of this book provide valuable evidence of the impact of different gender and faith perspectives on practical development issues while also highlighting the complexities and ambiguities of religious influences. Development workers, researchers and social activists will gain from these studies a greater awareness and more critical understanding of how different religious beliefs and practices, whether of Christianity, Buddhism or Islam in the Middle East, Asia, Africa or Latin America, can either be a potential barrier or alternatively a strong incentive for social change.'

Ursula King, Institute for Advanced Studies,
University of Bristol

'The collection's particular contribution is that it cautions that the links between religion, gender and development are always complex and sometimes contradictory, with ambiguous implications for realising gender equality. The nuanced analyses in the individual papers and the editor's contributions advance our understanding of the links between religion, gender and development in particular contexts and cultures.'

Carole Rakodi was Director of the Religions and Development Research Programme
from 2005 to 2010 and is currently Emeritus Professor in the International
Development Department, University of Birmingham.

Gender, Faith, and Development

Edited by Emma Tomalin
Series Editor Caroline Sweetman

Published by Practical Action Publishing Ltd in association with Oxfam GB

Practical Action Publishing Ltd
Schumacher Centre for Technology and Development
Bourton on Dunsmore, Rugby,
Warwickshire CV23 9QZ, UK
www.practicalactionpublishing.org

Oxfam GB,
Oxfam House, John Smith Drive,
Oxford OX4 2JY, UK

ISBN 978 1 85339 726 4

© Oxfam GB 2011

A catalogue record for this book is available from the British Library.

The contributors have asserted their rights under the Copyright Designs and Patents
Act 1988 to be identified as authors of their respective contributions.

Since 1974, Practical Action Publishing (formerly Intermediate Technology
Publications and ITDG Publishing) has published and disseminated books and
information in support of international development work throughout the world.
Practical Action Publishing Ltd (Company Reg. No. 1159018) is the wholly owned
publishing company of Practical Action Ltd. Practical Action Publishing trades only in
support of its parent charity objectives and any profits are covenanted back to Practical
Action (Charity Reg. No. 247257, Group VAT Registration No. 880 9924 76).

Oxfam is a registered charity in England and Wales (no 202918) and Scotland
(SCO 039042). Oxfam GB is a member of Oxfam International.

Cover photo: The mosque at Lampuuk, near Banda Aceh, which was hit badly by the
tsunami wave of December 2004. The community here decided to stay and rebuild as
soon as possible. A number of agencies decided to help this community to get started.
© Jim Holmes/Oxfam.

Indexed by Liz Fawcett, Harrogate, North Yorkshire
Typeset in Stone Serif by Bookcraft Ltd, Stroud, Gloucestershire
Printed by Hobbs the Printers Ltd
Printed on FSC 100% post-consumer waste recycled paper.

Contents

Chapter 1

Introduction

Emma Tomalin

The relationships between religion, gender, and development, are complex and context-specific. The need for development donors and organizations to consider religion as a relevant factor is ever more important, since religion and religious practices are a feature of life for the vast majority of women, men, and children whom development organizations seek to support. Engaging with religion, and understanding its role and significance in women's and men's lives, is also useful when this leads development policy-makers and practitioners to challenge the notion that 'development' can be reduced to the pursuit of economic prosperity alone, at the expense of other indicators of well-being. In addition, the gendered impact that development processes themselves can have on religious practices are significant, yet are typically overlooked in assessments and evaluations carried out by development actors.

The aim of this volume is to give an overview of published research in the field of religion, gender and development, to help those who are interested in promoting gender equality and women's rights in development understand this important topic.

Religion has, until recently, been largely ignored in development research, policy, and practice, due to the secular leanings of mainstream social science and development agendas (Selinger 2004: 526). One reason for this is an underlying assumption on the part of many secular development organizations that religion will disappear as societies modernize. Another is the belief that religion is a problem for development, supporting views about the world, and ways of living, that run counter to progressive and egalitarian development goals. Faith-based organizations (FBOs), such as Christian Aid, CAFOD, and Islamic Relief, have been an exception in an otherwise secular-oriented development environment. Over the past decade, this 'negative' engagement of development with religion has receded to some degree, and religious issues are being given more consideration, including in relation to women's rights and gender equality (Bradley 2006; 2010). This includes an increased willingness to support, fund and learn from those FBOs that have the experience and resources to lead secular organizations through examples of best practice.

About this book

This book brings together articles from three issues of the journal *Gender & Development*, together with an Introduction, Conclusion and Annotated bibliography.[1] In March 1999, *Gender & Development* published a thematic issue focusing on Religion and Spirituality: one of the first collections of articles to focus specifically on the complex links between religion, gender and development. A second issue, on the theme 'Working with faith-based communities', was published in November 2006.

The 1999 *G&D* volume captured a prior moment in the debate about religion, gender, and development, before the explosion of religion onto the global stage. The emphasis in it was very much on the reasons for the absence of religion in research, policy and practice about gender and development, and authors in the issue argued that there was a need for researchers, policy-makers and practitioners to begin to consider and address religion and religious institutions in their work on gender and women's rights.

The second *Gender & Development* issue, published in 2006, focused on working with faith-based organizations, and reflected the beginnings of a shift in attitude towards religion within governments and donors in the West. During the 2000s, in particular, interest in religion grew quickly within development organizations, and we saw an increase of funding from international donors to faith-based organizations, together with a desire to seek partnerships with faith leaders in pursuit of development goals (UNFPA 2004, 2010). Yet despite this new awareness and interest in religion and its relationship to gender equality and development, research into the impact of religion on women's lives and rights has been thin on the ground. The editorial to the 2006 volume noted: 'there is little scholarship or capturing of practice that considers the interaction between development practice and faith-based communities from the feminist perspective' (Greany 2006: 341). This research is needed to inform the kinds of work to be done with faith-based organizations. Today, this still remains an under-researched area.

In this Introduction, I will first present a short discussion introducing the field in more detail, with the aim of contextualizing the chosen chapters. Then I will guide the reader through the chapters, drawing out their main themes, and pointing towards more recent debates and controversies.

Ten chapters follow the Introduction. Readers will notice that four of the chapters focus on Islam (Adamu; Ahmed; Hopkins and Patel; Bartelink and Buitelaar), four on Christianity (Walker; Marshall and Taylor; Kane; Dolan), two deal with Buddhism (Tomalin; Saul) and one of the aforementioned also covers aspects of 'traditional religion' in Africa (Dolan).

In terms of research and writing on gender, religion and development, most attention has been paid to Islam. This can be seen in the context of the rise since '9/11' of global concern over fundamentalist[2] and extreme versions of Islam, and the specific implications of this for women's empowerment and development in different contexts. Several of the chapters in this volume explore this obsession with Islam by the West, which predates '9/11' but has intensified since. They argue that such an obsession results in a stereotyped depiction of Muslim women as particularly religious and as victims of a patriarchal and controlling Islamic faith (for example, Adamu; Bartelink and Buitelaar). While there is an absence of chapters in this volume that explore other faith traditions (including Hinduism and Sikhism), many of the themes that are covered in the selected chapters are relevant across faith traditions, and I will point readers to broader literature across regions and traditions in the accompanying annotated bibliography at the rear of this book.

At the end of the book, there is a short concluding chapter, in which I place the points raised in the introduction and through the chapters in a forward-facing context.

Contextualizing the field

The chapters in this volume suggest that there is a pressing need for development research, policy, and practice to adopt appropriate and sensitive ways of engaging with religious organizations and leaders in addressing gender concerns, and to ground their understandings of the ways that religion shapes gender roles and relationships in high-quality empirical research.

Development research, advocacy and community-level initiatives should be open to engaging with religion, and working with religious leaders and faith-based organizations, in order to deliver progressive change for women. Programmes that aim to pursue and secure women's rights have tended to ignore or reject religion, either for being irrelevant, or because patriarchal religious teachings and practices are considered to be one factor amongst many that contribute to women's unequal treatment.

At a time when the authority and appeal of conservative and fundamentalist religious outlooks seem to be on the rise in many contexts, exerting a particular influence on political systems, and often threatening women's control over their own bodies, concern about the fragility of women's rights is growing. Engagement with the religious institutions which shape gender roles and power relations in society is potentially an important step in addressing the negative effects of religion on women's lives.

As suggested above, the focus on religion and faith in the last decade has grown rapidly, and some commentators perceive development donors as having been in rather a hurry to engage with religious leaders and faith-based organizations, without a full awareness of the complexities and sensitivities involved in doing this (Pearson and Tomalin 2007). They argue that there is a risk that they actually collude with dangerous, essentialist ideas about women and gender roles and relations, while simultaneously cutting off the possibility of pursuing potentially more useful 'secular' strategies (see Bartelink and Buitelaar's chapter in this volume).

Religious feminism

A number of the chapters in this volume deal with the topic of 'religious feminism', and the role that it plays in women's empowerment and development at a local level. In some contexts, a 'secular' model of feminism has been rejected by development organizations and other civil society groups working in grassroots communities, perceiving it as lacking cultural relevance, due to its associations with the West. It is sometimes felt that in order to gain legitimacy within conservative religious cultures, the goal of gender equality needs to be pursued from within the religious worldview of women and men in that context. This has the potential to make development interventions more likely to be accepted, and, in the long term, more likely to be successful.

Interpretations of religious traditions that support gender equality have emerged from within religious traditions since the 1970s, in the guise of various 'feminist theologies'. Feminist researchers have engaged in the reinterpretation of religious texts and the traditions that surround them in order to uncover and promote understandings of religions that are gender equal. Acceptance of these interpretations has often been hampered by the lack of women scholars who are trained to undertake this sort of work. In addition, these scholars may be seen as elite, Western-influenced or -educated women, who have little connection with ordinary women.

In my own chapter, 'The Thai *bhikkhuni* movement and women's empowerment', I argue that styles of 'religious feminism' have emerged in different contexts, and from within different religious traditions that aim to reinterpret religious traditions in ways that promote equality and leadership roles. I suggest not only that this is relevant in order to improve the lives of 'religious' women (that is, those practising as nuns), but that it can also have a positive impact upon the roles and status of women more broadly. The research presented in the paper is concerned with the campaign to revive female ordination (*bhikkhuni* ordination) in Thailand. Many supporters of the campaign do not see a separation between the religious and the social, arguing that the powerful position of the orange-robed *bhikkhu* (monk) and negative stereotypes about women that are sustained by the Buddhist tradition (for example, according to Buddhist teachings, when people die they are thought to be reborn and if one is reborn as a woman it is viewed as the negative outcome of 'bad' actions in a previous life) do much to maintain 'broader social attitudes that increase women's vulnerability to risks such as domestic violence, sex trafficking or HIV' (p 44).

Some social movements and development interventions draw upon this feminist scholarship. The chapter by Fatima L. Adamu, 'A double-edged sword: challenging women's oppression within Muslim society in Northern

Nigeria', is also concerned with 'religious feminism' at the local level. Adamu argues that 'because gender issues are both religious and political concerns in many Muslim societies ... any attempt to reform gender relations that excludes religion is likely to fail' (97). The failure of international donors to incorporate Islam into gender policies and programmes has compounded the view that GAD ('gender and development') is a tool of the West and has meant that some of the principles adopted in international documents, such as CEDAW (the United Nations Convention on the Elimination of all forms of Discrimination Against Women) are perceived to be at odds with Islamic values about the family.[3] Muslim feminists who choose to pursue rights within Islam have found themselves trapped between conservatives in their tradition who deny women's rights in the name of religion and 'Western critics' who consider that in pursuing empowerment from within an Islamic framework they are ultimately 'accepting or supporting their own subordination' (98). While by the 1990s there was more of a willingness on the part of some international donors to fund Islamic NGOs working on women's and gender issues, the relationship between the two continues to be tense.

Bridget Walker's chapter 'Christianity, development, and women's liberation' also draws attention to the ambiguous role of religion in women's lives. As she highlights, religious teachings and institutions may legitimate oppression and violence, but may also provide women with sorely-needed resources in the struggle for emancipation and equality. Church is often a place where women can go to meet others, and also to escape from domestic abuse, and its teachings can be interpreted to support equality. Bridget Walker argues that development workers must be aware of these two options – domestication and liberation – and should be more accepting of the centrality of religion to women's lives, as well as the ways in which their religion may offer alternatives to 'conventional definitions of development as modernization and economic growth' (p66). This point is relevant to the critique that development agencies merely want to use religion instrumentally, to achieve their ends, rather than recognizing that it might challenge their goals and conception of development. It raises questions about the extent to which engagement with religion should force us to theorize or practise development differently and what trade-offs, compromises or tensions this throws up for the pursuit of gender equality (Deneulin and Bano 2009).

While many have welcomed the recent 'turn to religion' in development, others are concerned not to overestimate the role that 'religious feminisms' can play. As Mariz Tadros writes, 'caution is needed in assuming that a feminist re-engagement with religious text within a religious framework is a panacea for altering gender bias in laws, policies and practices' (2011: 9). This point is taken up in the chapter in this volume by Brenda Bartelink and Marjo Buitelaar, 'The challenges of incorporating Muslim women's views into development policy: analysis of a Dutch action research project in Yemen'. They discuss a development project in Yemen, funded by the Dutch government, which aimed to incorporate Muslim women's experiences into policy, based on an understanding of how women 'draw on religious and cultural resources to claim rights to reproductive health and education' (p14). The chapter demonstrates that even when women involved in the project were presented with feminist interpretations of the Koran, they were reluctant to use them and were just as likely as men to stick to traditional interpretations, perhaps as a reaction against perceived Western interference. Moreover, while women did see their religion as a source of comfort and support, this is arguably a 'discourse that potentially leads to acquiescence in oppressive situations' (p18). The authors make the important point that religion may well be able to support women's rights, but its ability to actually have an effect depends on the context. They conclude that the project set out to prove the assumption that Islam could empower women rather than to test it.

The above discussion suggests that there is no 'one size fits all' approach to incorporating 'religious feminism' into development. While it offers an alternative to Western secular feminism that is potentially more culturally appropriate, concerns about essentializing women's identities, and the privileging of a religious approach above others, urge caution.

Engaging with faith-based organizations and religious leaders: implications for gender and development

As discussed above, since the 1999 *Gender & Development* edition was published, there has been a greater engagement of Western donors with religion, through financing faith-based organizations and engaging with religious leaders. This 'global faith agenda' is potentially positive for women in the sense that it opens up a greater space for different sorts of religious feminisms in GAD work. However, the 'turn to religion' in development may have gender-related consequences, which have yet to be adequately considered by development practitioners and policy makers.

While religious traditions are neither uniformly misogynistic, nor incapable of reform, little evidence is available about the gender-related implications of current development policies and practical initiatives that actively engage with religion. There is a danger that the uncritical adoption of dominant (usually male) perspectives and voices within religious traditions may result in the marginalization of alternative voices and positions, for example feminist or gender-equal interpretations within religious traditions (Tomalin 2009). Also in prioritizing religion, other identities and alternative approaches may be ignored. For instance, there is some concern that well-established secular women's organizations are being sidelined by particular funding streams that favour faith-based organizations (FBOs), and by a general privileging of religiously-framed discourses (Patel 2011).

One of the perceived problems facing secular development organizations is wariness about being openly critical of religious organizations for their attitudes towards gender, or indeed probing very far at all into their values and policies on gender equality. However, in the absence of knowledge about these things, forming alliances with faith-based organizations could be detrimental to women's lives. The chapter in this book by Mandy Marshall and Nigel Taylor, 'Tackling HIV and AIDS with faith-based communities: learning from attitudes on gender relations and sexual rights within local evangelical churches in Burkina Faso, Zimbabwe, and South Africa', discusses the work of the UK-based Christian NGO, Tearfund, as it attempted to find out about and eventually challenge the attitudes of the evangelical churches in Africa on the issue of gender in the context of AIDS. Tearfund works through local evangelical Christian partner organizations in over 70 countries. The aim of this particular project was to establish the extent to which churches are dealing with issues around sexual activity and behaviour, and, if so, to ask whether they were undertaking this task in an informed and progressive manner. The study revealed, in particular, that the church teaches that women should serve and be subservient to men, and that this meant that they were typically unable to 'challenge the unfaithfulness of their husbands, or negotiate the use of a condom for safer sex' (p32). Overall, Tearfund was critical of the evangelical churches, a position that is perhaps easier for it to adopt as an 'insider' to the tradition. It funded a small pilot initiative to change attitudes. Projects such as this have the potential to be replicated in contexts where secular organizations find it difficult to gather information about the gender attitudes in particular religions, or to critique them when they are found to be problematic.

Religion and the control of women

The renewed public visibility of religion across the globe is tied up with the rise of fundamentalist or extremist religious outlooks. In the mainstream media, as well as in academic studies, most attention has been paid to Islam in this regard, with particular emphasis upon the use of Shari'ah law in certain contexts and the implications of this for women's human rights (Adamu). However, the use of religion to force women to conform to certain stereotypes is not just relevant for Muslim women. In India, for instance, a powerful nationalist movement has emerged that employs a fundamentalist and chauvinistic Hindu politics, which promotes particular religio-cultural identities for women as part of its claim to authentically represent the original Indian religiosity. The use of religious and cultural identities to mobilize political support that frequently results in violence has meant that both women and men have been engaged in violent acts against members of minority religious and ethnic communities (Burlett 1999; Sarkar and Butalia 1995; Sarkar 2001; Jeffery and Basu 1998).

In her chapter included this volume, 'Islam and development: opportunities and constraints for Somali women', Sadia Ahmed presents an account of the consequences for women of the rise of Islamic extremism in Somalia since the early 1990s. Under the influence of fundamentalist Islam, she notes an increase in certain practices, such as a rise in early marriage and polygamy, a desire for larger families, a decline in women's power in formal politics and an increased obligation to veil. Sadia Ahmed considers that the lack of religious education amongst the public means that they are unable to oppose the use of Islamic texts to oppress women, and, moreover, that Islamic extremists consider that women's movements are 'the central enemy', since fundamentalism is 'built upon the oppression of women'. While this indicates that the work on women's organizations must be significant, since it causes such concern to religious extremists, Sadia argues that 'their work is hindered by the lack of a coherent shared policy, and lack of access to the growing literature by Islamic scholars of both sexes, which challenges the denial of women's rights using religious texts'(p109).

One of the most concerning issues for women's rights activists has been the increasing opposition of conservative religious actors to reproductive rights.

As Shahra Razavi writes, this 'has been evident in the alliance forged between some Islamist states and the Vatican (in the context of the United Nations conferences of the 1990s) in opposition to the demands of global women's movements for gender equality, and most explicitly in reproductive and sexual rights' (2009: v). Moreover, the evangelical 'religious right' in North America was influential in the reinstatement of the 'Mexico City Policy' (also often referred to as the Global Gag Rule), by George Bush, on his first day in office in January 2001. The Mexico City Policy was first introduced by the Reagan Administration in 1984, but overturned by the Clinton Administration in 1993 and again repealed by President Obama in 2009. The Global Gag prohibited any organization in receipt of US funds from providing abortions (except in the cases of pregnancy from rape, incest or when a woman's life was in danger). The prohibition extended to offering advice and information about abortion services, and any lobbying activity for the legalization of abortion. This policy had a detrimental effect on the provision of reproductive and health services for women, far beyond the apparent curtailment of abortion-related services (Centre for Reproductive Rights, undated).

The chapter in this volume by Gillian Kane, 'Abortion law reform in Latin America: lessons for advocacy', looks at lessons that can be learnt for advocates and activists from recent changes in abortion policy in Mexico City, Colombia and Nicaragua (Sánchez Fuentes, Paine and Elliott-Buettner 2008). In the wake of the United Nations women's conferences of the 1990s, women's organizing for abortion rights intensified against the backdrop of opposition from the Catholic Church, with support from growing numbers of evangelical Protestants.

In Nicaragua, an alliance between Catholics and evangelical Protestants was influential in achieving an outright ban on abortion in 2006. However, what was most surprising was the shift in position of the former Sandanista president, Daniel Ortega, who had supported abortion during his reign in the 1980s and then during 2006 changed position to oppose abortion in order to gain Catholic votes in the election. By contrast, in Columbia and Mexico City the barriers erected by the Catholic Church in shifting 'the discourse from health, gender, and rights to religious considerations' (p116) were more successfully dismantled. While in Columbia the success was more modest, resulting in legislation in 2006 to permit 'therapeutic abortions', in Mexico City in 2007 all abortion became legal in the first trimester.

The chapter shows how, in some contexts, the use of international law to support arguments about reproductive health and rights can be effective in countering religious opposition. Nonetheless, the experience of Nicaragua demonstrates the need to be vigilant in the protection of even limited access to abortion. It also shows how political considerations may often trump support for women's rights, in contexts where the Church is powerful.

Taking religion into consideration in impact assessment

One of the main lessons from work undertaken on religion, gender and development to date is that the ways in which religions affect, and are affected by, gender relations are highly dependent on context. In this collection, the chapter by Adrienne Hopkins and Kirit Patel titled 'Reflecting on gender equality in Muslim contexts in Oxfam GB' presents a discussion about two Oxfam workshops held in 2004 and 2006. While respondents generally promoted the view that religion should be taken into consideration since there was a need to respond to local knowledge when approaching women's rights issues, they argued that it was also crucial not to prioritize religious identities over other identity markers or to assume that Muslim women were particularly religious.

The implications for development of this complex relationship between gender relations and religion depends very much on context. Moreover, situations can change very quickly, particularly in locations where the influence of fundamentalist religious forces can, in relatively short spaces of time, result in quite radical changes to laws and practices that restrict women's rights and freedoms. In Adrienne Hopkins and Kirit Patel's chapter, it was also stressed that when talking about 'Muslim contexts' 'we should bear in mind that contexts are constantly evolving, and that our understanding of context is both time- and place-specific, and subjective' (p54).

The fact that the terrain can shift quite quickly is borne out by comparisons drawn between the 2004 and the 2006 workshops. In particular, participants drew attention to the increasing politicization of Islam and that military action involving Western forces placed further pressure on many Muslim women. Under such difficult and tense circumstances strategies for engagement need to be ever more sensitive, cautious and contextual. While at certain times and in particular places engaging with religious texts and leaders can be a useful strategy in promoting female education or reproductive health, 'key allies' (including religious leaders or faith-based groups) need to be carefully identified to ensure that they too are committed to respecting people from diverse backgrounds, as well as the principle of gender equality.

The development process can itself also have an impact on religion, in terms of solidifying conservative reactions against women's rights agendas (when they are perceived as Western interference) or in bolstering the authority of patriarchal versions of traditions and male religious leaders (when engagement with religion is pursued without adequate appreciation of contextual factors). That religious considerations ought to be part of impact assessments is strongly suggested in the chapters by Catherine Dolan and Rebecca Saul. Catherine Dolan's chapter, 'Conflict and compliance: Christianity and the occult in horticultural exporting', describes the ways in which women turned to 'born again' Christianity, and also traditional witchcraft, in order to deal with conflicts over land, labour and income, created via the introduction of cash crops into Meru District, Kenya, in the early 1990s. In particular, women felt disadvantaged by the economic marginalization and overwork they have suffered as a result of the introduction of export crops. In response, some women turned to witchcraft, to inflict harm on their husbands, whereas others turned to Christianity to help them withstand the pressures they were under. Catherine Dolan argues that the struggles over land and labour were played out in the spiritual domain, yet the fact that too little attention has been paid by development practitioners to this aspect of people's lives meant that the impact of the development model used in Meru has not been fully understood.

Similarly, Rebecca Saul's chapter, 'No time to worship the serpent deities: women, economic change, and religion in north-western Nepal', explores how Buddhist rituals are changing in significance and nature in response to the growing tourist trade. In one settlement where tourism has had a limited impact, religious traditions have not been affected. However, in a neighbouring settlement that has engaged in tourism, women no longer have the time to carry out their traditional religious rituals. Rebecca Saul argues that assessments of women's work should also consider their spiritual roles and responsibilities. In common with Catherine Dolan, Rebecca Saul raises questions about the ways in which 'spiritual, reproductive, productive, and community roles support (or weaken) each other', and whether or not ideas of economic development and purchasing power ought to be 'the only yardsticks by which household and community well-being should be measured' (p95).

Conclusion

My aim in this introduction was to create a context for the chapters that follow, situating them within the broader debates about religion, gender and development. In the concluding chapter, my aim will be to consider the main themes raised in the introduction, in relation to the challenges of the future. What are the opportunities and pitfalls that are likely to be encountered by development researchers, policy makers and practitioners in negotiating the relationships between religion, gender and development? What tools and strategies might be employed to navigate this terrain? Where do we need to direct future research, so that engagement between development and religion can result in positive outcomes for women and gender equality?

Notes

1   Five of these ten chapters come from *Gender & Development* 7(1) (1999) and four from issue 14(3) (2006). One chapter has been included here from another issue 16(2) published in 2008 ('Reproductive Rights: Current Challenges'), for its contribution to the theme of this collection. The ten chapters in this book have been selected because, taken together, they present a good coverage of the areas of debate that have emerged in this field since the late 1990s. Moreover, several of the chapters point towards issues that have become of increasing concern since they were first published.

2   The term fundamentalist does not lend itself to a straightforward definition. When attached to the term 'religion' it is used to mean styles of religious belief and practice that endeavour to go back to the perceived fundamentals or basics of that particular tradition, often as a reaction against the corruption of the modern age. However, the term is not normally employed by those it is used to describe and tends to be used in a negative sense, typically with reference to forms of Islam. For these reasons there is sometimes a sense of discomfort with the term. Nonetheless, a number of scholars have argued that it is a useful concept pointing towards a modern phenomenon with shared characteristics across different religious traditions, including the control and symbolic idealization of women (Hawley and Proudfoot 1994: 27–30).

3   As other more recent work by Para-Mallam, Lanre-Abass, Adamu and Ajala (2011) has shown, the women's movement in Nigeria has failed in its bid to translate CEDAW (the Convention for the Elimination of all forms of Discrimination Against Women) into federal law in the country: at least partly because of the powerful influence of religious lobbies within both Islam and Christianity.

References

Bradley, Tamsin (2006) *Challenging the NGOs: Religion, Western Discourses and Indian Women.* London: I.B. Tauris.

Bradley, Tamsin (2010) *Religion and Gender in the Developing World: Faith-Based Organizations and Feminism in India.* London: IB Tauris.

Burlett, Stacey (1999) 'Gender relations, "Hindu" nationalism, and NGO responses in India'. *Gender & Development*, 7(1): 40–47.

Centre for Reproductive Rights Factsheet (undated) 'The Global Gag Rule's Effects on NGOs in 56 Countries', http://reproductiverights.org/en/document/the-global-gag-rules-effects-on-ngos-in-56-countries

Deneulin, Séverine with Masooda Bano (2009) *Religion in Development: Rewriting the Secular Script.* London: Zed Books.

Greany, Kate (2006) Editorial. *Gender & Development*, 14(3): 341–50.

Jeffery, Patricia and Amrita Basu (eds) (1998) *Appropriating Gender: Women's Activism and Politicized Religion in South Asia.* New York and London: Routledge.

Para-Mallam, Oluwafunmilayo J., Bolatito Lanre-Abass, Fatima Adamu , and Adebayo Ajala (2011) 'The Role of Religion in Women's Movements for Social Change: The Campaign for the Domestication of CEDAW in Nigeria', RaD Working Paper 59, University of Birmingham, Birmingham.

Patel, Pragna (2011) 'Cohesion, multi-faithism and the erosion of secular spaces in the UK: Implications for the human rights of minority women'. *IDS Bulletin.* 42(1): 26–40.

Pearson, Ruth and Emma Tomalin (2008) 'Intelligent design? A gender sensitive interrogation of religion and development'. In G. Clarke, Jennings and Shaw (eds) *Development, Civil Society and Faith-Based Organizations.* Basingstoke: Palgrave, pp. 46–71.

Razavi, Shahra (2009) 'Foreword'. In Jose Casanova and Anne Philips *A Debate on the Public Role of Religion and its Social and Gender Implications.* Gender and Development Programme Paper Number 5. UNRISD, pp. iii–v.

Sanchez Fuentes, María Luisa, Paine, Jennifer and Elliott-Buettner, Brooke (2008) 'The decriminalisation of abortion in Mexico City: How did abortion rights become a political priority?' *Gender & Development*, 16(2), 345–60.

Sarkar, Tanika and Urvashi Butalia (eds) (1995) *Women and Right-wing Movements: Indian Experiences.* London: Zed Books.

Sarkar, Tanika (2001) *Hindu Wife, Hindu Nation: Community, Religion, and Cultural Nationalism.* New Delhi and Bangalore: Permanent Black.

Selinger, Leah (2004) 'The forgotten factor: The uneasy relationship between religion and development'. *Social Compass*, 51: 523–43.

Tadros, Mariz (2011) 'Introduction: Gender, Rights and Religion at the Crossroads'. *IDS Bulletin*, 42(1): 1–9.

Tomalin, Emma (2009) 'Buddhist feminist transnational networks, female ordination and women's empowerment'. *Oxford Development Studies*, 37 (22): 81–100.

UNFPA (2004) *Culture Matters: Working with Communities and Faith-based Organizations: Case Studies from Country Programmes.* New York: UNFPA (http://www.unfpa.org/public/publications/pid/1430).

UNFPA (2010) *Culture Matters: Lessons from a Legacy of Engaging Faith-based Organizations.* New York: UNFPA (http://www.unfpa.org/public/pid/1353).

About the author

Emma Tomalin is Senior Lecturer, Department of Theology and Religious Studies, University of Leeds.

Chapter 2

The challenges of incorporating Muslim women's views into development policy: analysis of a Dutch action research project in Yemen

Brenda Bartelink and Marjo Buitelaar

This chapter first appeared in *Gender & Development* Volume 14, Issue 3, November 2006, pp. 351–62

This chapter discusses the Muslim Women and Development Action Research project (MWDAR), an attempt by the Dutch government to introduce new discourses on Islam and the empowerment of women into their development policy. Based on a discussion of the project in Yemen, an analysis of its evaluation reports, and follow-up research with project participants, we argue that the project did not meet expectations or project goals because it failed to go beyond an essentialist view of Muslim women. The chapter begins with a discussion of Dutch and Yemeni discourses on gender, Islam and development, and goes on to explore how these discourses ultimately influenced the project outcomes.

Introduction

'Let us do it our way.' This plea was made by Mariam Al-Schraiffe, an employee of the Women's Economic Empowerment Association (WEEA), a Yemeni organization working on the economic empowerment of women.[1] She made her remark during an interview with one of the authors of this chapter, in which she explained how many Yemenis frowned upon her organization for receiving financial support from the Netherlands. Organizations like WEEA have to steer a careful path between two opposing discourses on Muslim women. In the West, photographs of heavily veiled women feature in newspapers as images of repression, while those of Afghan women removing their *burqa* after the defeat of the Taliban have come to symbolize Muslim women's liberation. In Muslim countries, unveiling is interpreted by many as 'selling out to the West', while the headscarf has, amongst other things, come to stand for the rejection of Western imperialism and the defence of authentic Muslim culture.

'Let us do it our way' summarizes the difficulties that Muslim feminists face when taking a stance on debates on gender, Islam, and development. These debates are fuelled by worldwide feminist struggles against patriarchal and oppressive traditions and institutions on the one hand, and anti-colonial or anti-imperialist struggles on the other. In such discourses, women – and in this particular case, Muslim women – are used to express 'identity' and 'alterity' (otherness). In other words, the position of Muslim women is often used by Western commentators to point to the 'otherness' of Muslims, and by Muslims to pit 'the Muslim identity' against Western influences (Mahmood 2005; Baumann and Gingrich 2005). Muslim feminists challenge both kinds of essentialist discourse.[2]

The Muslim Women and Development Action Research project

The MWDAR project was initiated by the Netherlands Ministry of Foreign Affairs (MFA) in the 1990s, to gain a better understanding of how Muslim women caught between these discourses draw on religious and cultural resources to claim rights to reproductive health and education.[3] Religious resources may be certain Koranic texts, but also everyday religious knowledge, customs and rituals that influence choices concerning amongst other things marriage, pregnancy, contraception and the education of their daughters. The project also aimed to collect information on the empowerment strategies that individual Muslim women deploy in order to enhance their position and the freedom to exercise their rights. It was hoped that this would inform Dutch development policy on how to support these empowerment strategies in development cooperation, aiming to make Muslim women's views and ideas heard within the process.

Incorporating Muslim women's experiences into policy

Central to the research design was the idea that the analysis of the personal life stories and experiences of Muslim women would provide policy makers and development workers with tools to increase the suitability, impact and sustainability of development programmes working with Muslim communities.[4] The project involved a combination of desk- and field-based research within an action research design, including focus group discussions and life history interviews with poor women and men, and religious officials in urban and rural communities in Yemen. A key aim of the project was that it should be an entirely democratic and participatory process. As such, the training of Muslim women from the host countries as researchers, and their subsequent position as researchers working on the project was an important feature. However, the actual possibility for democratic and equal participation during the MWDAR project was significantly influenced by differences in power between actors in the project. We discuss this issue as we explore the Dutch and Yemeni discourses that shaped the MWDAR project.

Dutch discourses on women, Islam, and development

Dutch discourses on women, religion and development have been influenced by a number of factors.

The fact that the Netherlands is a highly secularized society has played a significant role in shaping the debate on the role of religion in development (Buijs 2004). This debate is characterized by two contradictory discourses: one depicts religion as a vehicle of social change and development, the other as a barrier to such processes. Popular belief in the Netherlands tends towards the view that religion, and especially Islam, can frequently act as a barrier to positive change for women. For example, Dutch media coverage of the Iranian Revolution in 1979 and its aftermath highlighted the detrimental effects of measures that were imposed on women by the Islamic government. Ongoing public debate on the integration of immigrants to the Netherlands into Dutch society has reinforced this opinion, as this debate has often been characterized by a focus on the position of Muslim women, who are frequently portrayed as the victims of an oppressive religion.

Dutch development policy makers have been preoccupied with the issue of Muslim women and development for some time. When, in 1991, the then Dutch Minister for Development Cooperation, Jan Pronk, declared 'autonomy' as the focus of his development policy, questions were asked in the Dutch Parliament on the applicability of this policy in Muslim societies, given the assumed subordinate position of women in those societies (Ministry of Foreign Affairs 1991). In reaction to these discussions, research was undertaken with the aim of analysing the position of women in several Muslim countries receiving Dutch aid, and investigating the feasibility of programmes aimed at increasing the autonomy of Muslim women. The research report concluded that, while the actual position of many women in Muslim countries was indeed a reason for concern, religious influence played only a minor role in comparison to socio-economic factors. The case studies suggested that women were primarily concerned with the severe poverty they suffered, and their struggle for their own and their children's health. The research also gave an overview of women's rights according to authoritative Islamic texts and concluded that these texts allowed for interpretations that could enhance the autonomy of women (Jansen et al. 1994), and lead to their empowerment, thus seeming to dispel the essentialist idea that Islam automatically results in the oppression of women.

Following this research, several meetings and seminars were organized by the MFA to discuss the position of women within Muslim societies, and their portrayal in Islamic texts. During this time, the work of the Pakistani Muslim feminist theologian, Riffat Hassan, in particular contributed to the development of a view on the potential for Islam to play a positive role in Muslim women's lives.[5] Hassan (1998) argues that because of Islam's position 'at the heart of Muslim identity' it could be an appropriate and powerful vehicle for the promotion of women's rights and empowerment.

It was partly this argument that led to the establishment of the MWDAR project, with a remit to explore further exactly how Islam could be a tool for the promotion of Muslim women's rights. But this is an argument that, we argue later, is partly flawed.

Yemeni discourses on women, gender, and development

Gender is a very sensitive issue in Yemen, as many activists from Yemeni women's organizations and development agencies interviewed in the research for this chapter explained. After the unification of Yemen and the ensuing civil war, bilateral donors and international organizations began to give considerable financial development support to the country. Some of this money was earmarked for women's organizations and projects, and with it came the condition that the Yemeni government report on the status of women in Yemen and on its efforts to improve it. From the outset, the debate on gender and development was, therefore, associated by many Yemenis with Western interference.

This led to some tension, illustrated well by the controversy over the Empirical Research and Women's Study Centre (ERWSC), an example given by a number of interviewees during the MWDAR project. The ERWSC was established at Sana'a University in 1996 with Dutch government funding to focus on Yemeni gender studies. Through its various courses, PhD projects and seminars, the centre introduced a new academic discourse on gender and Islam. In 1999, an ERWSC conference on women's studies resulted in heated debate, when one of the speakers addressed the sensitive topic of *ijtihad*, the free and rational interpretation of the Koran, which aims to accommodate Koranic views and prescriptions to specific situations and changes in everyday life. The speaker at the ERSCW conference (in line with the influential Islamic theological works of early modernists and several present-day feminist scholars such as Riffat Hassan) openly criticized the interpretations of the classical religious authorities.

After the conference, there was a considerable backlash. Rumours spread that the ERWSC wished to rewrite the Koran, the centre was harshly criticised in newspaper articles and in Friday sermons in mosques, and the ERWSC director was personally attacked and threatened with excommunication. Against this backdrop, the Dutch government took the decision to withdraw funding and close the centre. Even after the closure, newspapers continued to state that the so-called 'genderists' had come to Yemen to undermine its Islamic morality and traditions. Criticism towards the presumed hidden agendas of donors and the influence of globalization and Western feminism fuelled a discourse in which Western feminism was 'demonized' (Badran 2000). The MWDAR project, which dealt explicitly with the sensitive issues of Islam and the position of women, was clearly affected by this context. Implemented between 1999 and 2001, when the controversy reached a climax, and like the ERWSC, funded by the Dutch government, it was open to the same criticisms, and to accusations of interference. It is strange, therefore, that neither the ERWSC controversy nor its possible effects on the MWDAR project are mentioned in the project reports.

Yemeni women's life stories

Despite the precarious situation that formed the backdrop to the implementation of MWDAR, as many as 76 women consented to be interviewed for the research, and another 65 participated in focus group discussions. In addition, 53 men were interviewed, including a number of local religious officials (KIT & Women and Development Division, MFA 2001b: annex 1.1). Islam was addressed both in relation to education and reproductive health, and as a separate topic. The reports of the interviews and discussions provide a rich overview of Yemeni women's lives in the rural Dhamar Governorate and in the city slums of Aden and Dhamar city. These interviews yielded a huge amount of valuable information on women's experiences as daughters, wives, and mothers, and on their choices regarding education and reproductive health.

One example is the story of Ebtissam, a young woman from Dhamar. Ebtissam and her sister were given in marriage to the two sons of an uncle in Sana'a, where Ebtissam gave birth to a baby girl.[6] She recounted how she and her sister were treated harshly by their in-laws, and how she was forced to work long hours with little to eat as the family's housekeeper. She finally took the brave step of running away when she was punished for protesting at the physical abuse experienced by her sister. This excerpt from an interview with Ebtissam describes her experience:

> They besieged us and locked us up. I woke up early and did the dawn prayers. At six in the morning I collected the garbage and did as if I was bringing it to the garbage container ... I went to the neighbours and called our house. I told [my parents], they are locking us up and that they had beat my sister up ... God answered my mother's prayers and we got divorced ... I went crying to my husband's house as a bride and came back laughing to my parents' house as a divorcee. (KIT & Women and Development Division, MFA 2001b: 64)

Ebtissam was forced to leave her daughter with her ex-husband who told the girl that her mother had died. Eventually, Ebtissam had a chance to meet her daughter, only to find that her daughter did not recognize or accept her. Although it hurt her deeply that she could not take care of her daughter herself, she refused to return to her in-laws. Weeping bitterly, she told the interviewer how she was eventually granted visitation rights to see her daughter.

Faith as a coping strategy or Islam as a tool for empowerment?

What does this excerpt show us about Ebtissam's responses to the difficulties she faces, the power – or lack of power – she has, and the role, if any of religion? The story certainly seems to contain episodes in which she was able to make choices and negotiate between her needs and wishes and the expectations of others (her daughter, her in-laws and her own family), for example, in her active decision to run away. What stands out most, perhaps, are the extraordinarily harsh living conditions in which she was kept by her in-laws. Like Ebtissam, most of the women interviewed spoke of facing extreme poverty, illness, exclusion, and gender discrimination.[7]

Most notable in the MWDAR Yemen Country Report are the depictions of women's endeavours to create meaningful lives in particularly harsh circumstances. Given the project's focus on religion, however, it is remarkable that Islam seems to play such a minor role in the life stories recounted by interviewees. Although Ebtissam, for example, explained her successful efforts to get a divorce in terms of God answering her mother's prayers, her story centres on the abuse by her in-laws and the difficulties she encounters as a divorcee and mother. In fact, there is little evidence in the MWDAR reports to suggest that the women interviewed see Islam as playing an important role in their own empowerment. What does come through, however, is that women find religion to be predominantly a source of comfort and support and that they experience their faith independently from institutionalized Islam, as this excerpt from one of the reports highlights:

> They [Muslim women interviewees] have hope! One woman told us [the report's authors] that she talks to God all the time. Sometimes she asks him 'Why, why did you make my life like this?' There is a communication direct to the God, to Allah. That means that they have a direct religion and don't depend on their husbands.[8]

Based on this recognition of women's faith as a coping strategy, the reports subsequently identify Islam as an important resource for women's empowerment. However, we question this leap of logic, and argue that it is based on a misunderstanding of the concept of 'empowerment'. While trust in God clearly appears to help the interviewees to endure precarious situations, this coping strategy lacks the element of 'moving into positions of power' that is central to the concept of empowerment (Rowlands 1998). Empowerment, we argue, involves the ability to make one's own choices and to develop strategies to change imbalances in power relations, something that a 'coping strategy mechanism' does not have the potential to do. In this sense, unlike the report authors, we see coping strategies not as a form of empowerment for Muslim women, but as a discourse that potentially leads to acquiescence in oppressive situations.

Women's rights and the interpretation of the Koran

A second way in which Islam may contribute to the 'empowerment' of women, based on the idea of the interpretation of the Koran, is also discussed in the MWDAR Yemen reports. The reports state that, on the one hand, interpretations of the Koran promoted by religious leaders and Yemeni men in general 'more often than not … support the status quo and inflect those aspects of gender roles and relations that support and cohere with the patriarchal traditions of the wider culture' (KIT & Women and Development Division, MFA 2001a: 11). In this context, the reports argue that access to interpretations of '[mainstream] religious resources … which support the rights of women to control over their bodies and fertility is crucial'. This argument is supported by recounting the life story of Husn, a young middle-class woman who tells the interviewers that she claims her right to practise birth-control on the basis of certain interpretations of the Koran (KIT & Women and Development Division, MFA 2001b: 24, 87). Although this is the only example that the researchers came across, from it they conclude that religious education, which 'has always been considered outside the purview of development activities', is an essential strategy for promoting women's access to interpretations of the Koran that support gender equality.

However on the other hand, the reports also acknowledge that having access to religious knowledge is in itself no guarantee that women will champion women's rights. This is illustrated by the life story of Fathia, a middle-class teacher who tells interviewers that she often refers to Koranic texts to support strict sex-segregation and to condemn the use of contraceptives (KIT & Women and Development Division, MFA 2001b: 22). Both these women are educated, independent women, who, rather than relying on male interpretations of the Koran, are able to interpret the text for themselves, and yet they come up with entirely opposing interpretations. Although Fathia represents the articulate, educated woman the MWDAR project researchers perhaps imagined as a role model when they suggested increased religious education as a means to women's empowerment, her interpretations of Koranic texts are quite different from what the researchers had envisaged. Hence the reports' caveat that the religious education provided to women should include information and knowledge that support gender equality, and thereby the empowerment of women.

In the discussion around religious education and the potential for women's rights to be realized through reinterpretation of the Koran, the MWDAR reports appear to neglect the way in which Dutch and Yemeni discourses on gender and Islam are embedded in postcolonial power relations, and how this impacts on the potential for women's empowerment through religion. As we discussed earlier in the chapter, for many Muslims in Yemen and elsewhere, defending the presumed 'traditional' position of women has come to symbolize resistance to and rejection of Western influences, and the defence of Islam's authenticity. This should not be underestimated, and women are just as likely to take up this defence as others. Against this background, Dutch involvement in educational programmes promoting interpretations of the Koran that openly oppose dominant patriarchal interpretations could prove to be highly problematic, if not counter-productive. This might explain why there has not been any follow-up to the MWDAR project and why, two years after it ended, the various actors interviewed by us were not able to indicate any actual outcomes of the project.

Failing to go beyond essentialist discourses

The MWDAR project therefore seems to have been based on false premises, characterized by an essentialist view of Islam and an inadequate understanding of the role of religion in power relations between the Netherlands as a powerful and influential donor and Yemen as a recipient of development aid. Education, and enabling women to interpret religious texts freely, may result in the promotion of women's rights. But the fact that these 'free' interpretations may continue to deny women's rights illustrates that there is nothing intrinsic in Islam that is capable of changing gendered power relations. Muslims draw on Islamic texts, rituals and symbols to construct narratives and make claims about 'pure' Islam. However, every Islamic discourse is embedded in a particular socio-economic, historical and political context, like the one we have described in Yemen. Whatever comes to be accepted as 'the true Islam' in a given context is the outcome of struggles over power between (groups of) people occupying different societal positions, with different interests (Assad 1993; Baumann 1999). So for instance, the controversy around the ERWSC was rooted not only in heated debate on alternative interpretations of the Koran and whether such reinterpretation is or is not allowed in 'true Islam', but also in suspicions regarding the influence of the Netherlands government that funded the ERWSC, with the consequence that it had more money than some other faculties of Sana'a University. Although Islam may indeed lie 'at the heart' of many Muslim women's identities, as Riffat Hassan suggests, this does not mean that the situation in which these women find themselves can be explained or changed in terms of Islam or 'Islamic culture' only. Therefore, any development efforts to address their situations need to go beyond their identity as 'Muslim women'.

Discussion and conclusion

The inadequate understanding of the role of religion in society and the failure to analyse the ways in which different discourses on Islam are socio-economically and politically embedded goes some way to explaining why the outcomes of the MWDAR project did not meet its goal of incorporating new, empowering discourses on Islam and women into Dutch development policy. As we have shown, in some cases conclusions were drawn which did not reflect the actual findings, based on the preconceived assumptions of

Western researchers about the significance of the role of Islam for women in Yemen. In fact, conceived in the context of Dutch discourses on women and Islam, the project was premised on the assumption that Islam could play an empowering role, and appears to have set out to prove this point rather than explore it. As such, one of the key recommendations in the final report, to buttress or even promote the education of women in interpretations of Islam that foster empowerment, expressed a view on how Islamic doctrine could be used to enhance Muslim women's empowerment, but did not reflect the actual research findings.

As we argued earlier, the dominant Dutch discourse on development cooperation in Muslim countries is influenced by domestic 'Islamicized' discourses on multiculturalism and the integration of migrants in the 1990s. Echoing the former European colonial narrative on Islam the issue of women has once more emerged as the centrepiece of the debate (Ahmed 1992: 150).[9] For many Dutch citizens, women's presumed subordinate position, symbolized by the headscarf, represents the 'backwardness' of Islam, in terms of women's rights. In an attempt to rectify this one-sided view, others emphasize the potential of Islam as a source of inspiration, emancipation and empowerment.

We have shown that the problem with both discourses is that they are characterized by an essentialist view of Muslim women, who are defined first and foremost in terms of the religious dimension of their identity. What is more, what is identified as 'Islamic' is wrongly represented as something that affects all Muslim women in the same way. Regardless of whether Islam is perceived as a barrier to, or vehicle of, social change and development, in either view Muslim women are treated as a homogeneous group.

This runs counter to the principles of the internationally accepted discourses on gender and development, which explicitly recognize the diverse and multiple identities of women (Brouwers 2001). The strong focus on the religious dimension of the identity of Yemeni women precluded an adequate analysis of the complexity of the context in which these women experience poverty, illness, and exclusion. Although the explicit goal of the project was to make women's voices 'authoritative' in Dutch development cooperation, as it turned out, these voices were – at least partially – muted. From the onset, the initiators of the MWDAR project were convinced they knew what the right course for the development and empowerment of Muslim women would be and, it seems, failed to listen to those voices they were aiming to make heard.

This analysis has shown that development cooperation is firmly rooted not only in development practice itself, but also in political and public discourses in donor and developing countries. In any development context, it is therefore necessary to critically analyse dominant discourses on women, religion, and development cooperation, because these discourses foster power differences and enhance exclusion. Because of its powerful position, the development donor has a special responsibility to reflect on its own agenda, to be open to dialogue and debate, and to be aware of unequal power relationships with the recipients of its aid. Only when these factors have been taken into account can the plea to 'Let us do it our way' be heard and recognized as a request for respect and recognition of the ways that Yemeni women are empowering themselves, not only as Muslims but as strong women with diverse identities.

Notes

1   This chapter is based on an analysis of the MWDAR project reports (see note 3) as well as follow-up research, during which we interviewed Dutch and Yemeni women who had been involved in the MWDAR project, as well as Yemeni women activists from several women's and development organizations. For reasons of privacy we either use pseudonyms for our interviewees, or we identify them only by their relation to the project.

2   In an essentialist view, cultures or religions are presented as coherent, integrated, organic wholes with clear-cut boundaries that consist of fixed norms and practices adopted by a homogeneous community.

3   The MWDAR project was set up in six countries: Bangladesh, Ethiopia, Mali, Senegal, Sudan, and Yemen. The project resulted in seven country reports, one of which focused on Yemen, and a synthesis report in which the most important findings were summarized. For the purposes of this chapter, we discuss the project outcomes from Yemen only. The references section specifies which report is being referred to when, but for the purposes of readability, we have referred to 'the reports' throughout the text.

4   Unpublished project proposal, MFA. In the synthesis report this is summarized in a more general manner: 'to develop approaches to gender and development' (1).

5   Hassan was one of the keynote speakers at the 1996 conference The Power of Culture, organized by UNESCO and the Dutch government (NEDA). Her speech on global ethics and cultural diversity can be found at: http://kvc.minbuza.nl/uk/archive/amsterdam/ukverslag_hassan.html (last accessed 3 May 2006).

6   Interview Al Faruqi, December 2004; Country report Yemen: The story of Ebtissam has also been analysed by Leydesdorff (2004) who shows that although women often shape their lives within the boundaries of tradition, they do not necessarily lack autonomy.

7   This is shown in the summary of findings in each area, which gives figures indicating birth and loss of children and presents seven fully transcribed life stories.

8   Interview Al-Faruqi, December 2004.

9   As Leila Ahmed has demonstrated, in the eyes of the British colonizers, veiled Muslim women symbolized the backwardness of Egypt. The endeavour to improve the position of women was used to legitimize British colonial rule. As a reaction to this, in liberation and later nationalist Middle Eastern discourses, women came to symbolize the virtuous Islamic identity or the modernity of the new nation state (Ahmed 1992).

References

Ahmed, L. (1992) *Women and Gender in Islam: Historical Roots of a Modern Debate*, Yale University Press, New Haven, London.

Assad, T. (1993) *Genealogies of Religion*, Johns Hopkins University Press, Baltimore

Badran, M. (2000) 'Gender: meanings, uses and discourses in post-unification Yemen', *Yemen Times* (25, 26, 27), Sana'a, 9 June–9 July.

Baumann, G. (1999) *The Multicultural Riddle: Rethinking National, Ethnic and Religious Identities*, Routledge, New York, London

Baumann, G. and Gingrich, A. (2005) *Grammars of Identity/Alterity: A Structural Approach*, Berghahn Books, New York, Oxford

Brouwers, R. (ed) (2001) 'Partners (m/v) in ontwikkelingssamenwerking: Helpt hulp ook vrouwen?' In Schulpen, L. (ed) *Hulp in Ontwikkeling: Bouwstenen voor de Toekomst van Internationale Samenwerking*, Koninklijke van Gorcum, Assen

Buijs, G., (2004) 'Religion and Development'. In Salemink, O., van Harskamp, A. and Giri, A. Kumar (eds) *The Development of Religion/The Religion of Development*, Eburon Publishers, Delft.

Hassan, R. (1998) 'Gelijk voor God, ongelijk op aarde? Islamitische vrouwen en mensenrechten'. In Noordam, K., van Oordt, R. and Çörüz, Ç. (eds) *Mensen, Rechten en Islam: Beschouwingen over Grondrechten*, Uit-geverij Bulaaq/SBLI , Amsterdam.

Jansen, W. et al. (1994) 'Women and Islam in Muslim Societies, Poverty and Development. Analysis and Policy' Ministry of Foreign Affairs, Development Cooperation Information Department (DVL/OS), The Hague.

KIT & Women and Development Division, Ministry of Foreign Affairs, the Netherlands (2001a) 'Muslim Women and Development Action Research Project: Synthesis Report', KIT Publishing, Amsterdam.

KIT & Women and Development Division, Ministry of Foreign Affairs, the Netherlands (2001b) 'Muslim Women and Development Action Research Project: Country Report Yemen', KIT Publishing, Amsterdam.

Leydesdorff, S. (2004) *De Mensen en de Woorden: Geschiedenis op Basis van Verhalen*, Meulenhoff, Amsterdam

Mahmood, S. (2005) *Politics of Piety: The Islamic Revival and the Feminist Subject*, Princeton University Press, Princeton

Ministry of Foreign Affairs (1991) *A World of Difference*, Directorate General for International Cooperation, Ministry of Foreign Affairs, The Hague

Rowlands, J. (1998) 'A word of the times, but what does it mean? Empowerment in the discourse and practice of development' in Afshar, H. (ed) *Women and Empowerment. Illustrations from the Third World*, Palgrave Macmillan, New York.

About the authors

Brenda Bartelink was a policy advisor on gender and reproductive health at the MFA and was involved in the UNFPA/MFA international conference 'Cairo and Beyond: Reproductive Rights and Culture'. In 2004 she did field-work on the empowerment of women in Yemen, part of MA research in which she analysed discourses on women, Islam and development cooperation. Currently she is working on a PhD research project on religion and develop-ment cooperation at Groningen University, the Netherlands.

Marjo Buitelaar is Associate Professor of Contemporary Islam and Methodology of Qualitative Social-Science Research in the Faculty of Theology and Religious Studies at Groningen University, the Netherlands. She was a consultant to a Dutch-funded Primary Health Care Project in Yemen in the 1980s and is co-author of the MFA report 'Women in Development in Muslim Countries: Negotiating a Better Future' (1993).

Chapter 3

Tackling HIV and AIDS with faith-based communities: learning from attitudes on gender relations and sexual rights within local evangelical churches in Burkina Faso, Zimbabwe, and South Africa

Mandy Marshall and Nigel Taylor

This chapter first appeared in *Gender & Development* Volume 14, Issue 3, November 2006, pp. 363–74

The AIDS pandemic in Africa is devastating the continent. The institution of marriage does not appear to be protecting women – in some countries rates of infection among married women are higher than those among unmarried, sexually active women. Recognizing that unequal gender relations are a driving force behind the AIDS pandemic, this chapter explores the position of local evangelical churches in Africa with respect to gender relations and sex, and the implications for HIV and AIDS. Based on desk and field research carried out by the UK-based NGO Tearfund, the findings indicate that these churches were largely silent on the issue of gender and sex, or were reinforcing traditional values which contribute to HIV infection. In a number of countries, the church seems to have failed to provide leadership to young people, especially young women, facing huge pressure to be sexually active. Strategies for responding are outlined.

In some heavily affected countries, married women have higher rates of HIV infection than their unmarried, sexually active peers.
Kofi Annan, UN Secretary General, World AIDS Day 2004

Adhering to the teachings of the Church, we determined to engage more deeply in challenging cultures and traditions which stifle the humanity of women and deprive them of equal rights. We agreed that our greatest challenge is to nurture and equip our children to protect themselves from HIV, so that we can fulfil the vision of building a generation without AIDS.
Pastoral letter from the Primates of the Anglican Communion,
27 May 2003

All the pastors' wives had never seen a condom as it is seen as a tool for unfaithful wives.

NGO worker, Burkina Faso

Introduction

The AIDS pandemic is having a devastating effect on Africa, with over 2 million deaths in 2005, and 24 million people living with HIV, of whom nearly 60 per cent are women. The impact of the pandemic is heavily gendered: one of the groups most vulnerable to HIV infection is married women. In addition, girls and women often bear the heaviest of burdens in caring for the sick and affected, and women living with HIV often suffer blame and rejection by their families and communities. At the same time, Christianity is seeing an unprecedented period of expansion in Africa, particularly of evangelical[1] and Pentecostal churches, which now have an estimated 70 million adherents.

Against this backdrop, Tearfund wanted to find out if, or how, the evangelical church in Africa is speaking out on the issue of gender in the context of AIDS, or whether it is staying silent, so reinforcing the perception that it accepts traditional values. Are churches tackling the delicate issues of sexual activity and behaviour, and if so, is this being done in an informed and positive manner? Tearfund therefore funded a small research project to assess the current situation with regards to gender, HIV and AIDS and the role of the church in three African countries. The aim of the project was to discover:

1   Were churches doing any work in this area?
2   If so, how successful was it proving to be?
3   What lessons could be learnt?

Tearfund's mission and values significantly informed its decision to undertake research in this area, and its choice of approach.[2] The organization was founded in 1968 in response to an increasing demand from evangelical Christians in the UK (who total more than 1 million) for a way to address the needs of the world's poor. Tearfund is now one of the seven largest UK-based international development NGOs, working in over 70 countries in Latin America, Asia, and Africa through local evangelical Christian partner organizations. The organization's distinctive approach is that it draws on Christian resources and values as an integral part of its relief and development work. Its organizational purpose is to follow the teachings of Jesus Christ in enabling those who share evangelical Christian beliefs to bring good news to poor communities.

For Tearfund, this foundation translates into:

- Ensuring that Christians are aware of the call to address poverty;
- Effective action to bring about sustainable responses to need;
- Speaking out with, and on behalf of, poor people, to bring about justice.

The latter includes gender justice. Tearfund believes that men and women are equal before God and that men and women are to work in partnership with one another.[3] Tearfund is committed to the vision of the restoration of God's original intention of partnership for man and woman[4] and is concerned that the wider evangelical constituency should understand, and act upon, these principles, especially in the context of HIV and AIDS.

Tearfund seeks to challenge and support evangelicals to respond to poverty through direct action for poor people and through speaking out to inform and influence. In particular, Tearfund believes that the church can be, and in many places is, a positive influence for change as it is often well respected and listened to within communities.

Carrying out the research

The research was done in two distinct phases – firstly, desk-based research gave a broad overview of the role being played by the evangelical church in Africa, and highlighted areas that we wanted to probe in more depth at local level. The desk-based research also informed the choice of fieldwork locations: South Africa, Zimbabwe and Burkina Faso.

The field research visited a range of NGOs and churches, of which some were current Tearfund partners and others were not. We conducted semi-structured interviews with key staff in organizations working with the church. Ten organizations were interviewed in South Africa, seven in Zimbabwe and seven in Burkina Faso. In many cases, Tearfund partners facilitated visits to rural communities to interview pastors and members of the church about their views on the subject. During the interviews it was often necessary to separate the men and women in order to gain an openness and honesty in the answers.

Having completed the fieldwork, we presented an initial analysis of the information to the partners, Christian AIDS Taskforce (CAT) in Zimbabwe, and Vigilance in Burkina Faso, giving them an opportunity to correct any wrong perceptions we might have gained. We also held workshops to present the initial findings to country staff from a range of other Christian NGOs and to ask for their feedback. Workshop participants were asked to identify the issues, barriers and solutions to working with the church on gender and HIV and AIDS. These discussions were used in the analysis of the results for triangulation purposes.

Findings of the desk-based research

The link between gender and HIV and AIDS

Gender is one of the keys to the response to AIDS in Africa, because it is often the imbalance in power relations between men and women that drives the spread of HIV through heterosexual relationships. This is seen in individual relationships, and in the attitudes towards gender within society. Furthermore, a key issue confronting African society in general, and the church in particular, is the nature of the relationship in marriage between a husband and wife. Whilst it is recognized that for many African women, marriage is what a woman aspires to, paradoxically, marriage is a key risk factor for women to become infected with HIV. This is because their husbands may already be infected, or become infected as a result of extra-marital sex, and because for a variety of reasons, condoms are rarely used for safer sex.

The gendered nature of HIV and AIDS is borne out in a number of other practices where men put women and girls at risk of infection, such as widow inheritance[5] and 'offering' women as a sign of hospitality.[6] Although most practices that increase women's risk of infection are driven by beliefs about the sexual role of men, women's beliefs about their own roles also contribute to some extent. Girls are brought up to believe that they should seek to satisfy the sexual needs of their husband rather than expect mutual sexual satisfaction. This may result in support for practices such as 'dry sex',[7] and female circumcision. Young women have sexual relationships with older men – 'Sugar Daddies' – who give them presents, while they also have a partner of their own age. In addition, poverty often forces women into risky sexual relations.

The underlying cause of this situation is the way in which women and girls in parts of Africa are socially subordinate to, and economically dependent upon, men. Contemporary non-church culture can endorse the view that men are dominant and are expected to have several partners. Women are expected to be submissive and passive. They are often economically dependent on men and are therefore in a weak position to negotiate about sexual matters, or to challenge extra-marital relationships. Women have little control over whether, where, and how sexual relations take place. Anecdotal evidence from South Africa also suggests that social change and ongoing high levels of poverty and unemployment appear to have a particular effect on the male psyche, which in turn impacts on women's vulnerability to HIV. With a man unable to articulate his masculinity by providing for his family, or having status from a job, he may look even more to demonstrate it through his sexual prowess with multiple, concurrent partners.

Evangelical churches and gender and HIV and AIDS

There is a widely held view that in sections of the evangelical churches, conservative attitudes towards sex and women are more entrenched than in society as a whole. Church leaders and members believe, in some cases, that sex is to be endured rather than enjoyed as a gift from God, that it is inappropriate, within culture, to speak about sex, and that the Bible requires women to be submissive. These views are mutually reinforcing. The reluctance to speak about sexual issues means that the church is perceived to agree with traditional values. This makes it difficult for a woman church member to challenge her husband's extra-marital affairs. Many churches associate condoms with promiscuity and so speak against their use, even for safer sex within marriage.

Cultural issues seem to reinforce, and are in some cases reinforced by, evangelical attitudes. The interrelationship is such that it demands that we address not only African cultural traditions and their impact on HIV and AIDS, sex and gender relations, but also challenge the church on its position on the issues. Evangelical beliefs can compound the situation when an incomplete knowledge or biased selection of biblical texts leads to an unbalanced view. For example, many Christians are familiar with only selected biblical texts that refer to the submission of women, and neglect to balance this with other texts that speak of the necessity of equal submission to one another in love, and of men and women being created equally in the image of God. African Christians suggest that in Africa many who identify as Christians actually operate in two worlds concurrently: 'Christian Western civilization', and underneath, traditional African culture. Often, it is traditional values that define beliefs around gender and sex for Christian men and women.

Given this background, it is perhaps unsurprising that when asked about working with the church in the community, several Christian NGOs implied that progress in changing attitudes to gender is slow and frustrating, particularly with leaders of evangelical churches. To explore these initial findings further, and to investigate the reality of working with the local church on issues of HIV and AIDS and gender, we moved on to our fieldwork. This included visits to Mthatha and Pietermaritzburg in South Africa, Bulawayo in Zimbabwe and Ouagadougou in Burkina Faso. In the next section we discuss our findings from our research in these places.

Reality at community level

South Africa

Our fieldwork in South Africa highlighted the disturbing situation of many young people. They are faced with pressures from a number of sources, for example, from Western-orientated media, to attain the trappings of prosperity, but at the same time have few prospects of a secure livelihood. They are watching their parents and siblings die of AIDS. Parents are no longer setting boundaries. With little sense of purpose or hope, they turn to sex for recreation or a measure of intimacy without concern for their own prospects of becoming infected. In addition, post-apartheid freedom has resulted here in the misinterpretation of democracy as 'anything goes'. With this new-found freedom has come a general rejection of boundaries and any frameworks that appear to limit freedom, including biblical teaching. Although it is estimated that approximately half of the youth attend church, the teaching received seemingly has little impact on their lives and their sexual behaviour. Even among the youth found within churches, there are many who are sexually active (Mash and Kareithi 2005). HIV prevalence continues to increase in many provinces.

In this context, there is considerable pressure on young women to have sex without condoms, stemming from a range of factors including peer pressure, economic situations, thrill and excitement, and simply wanting a baby. A common phrase reportedly used by teenagers in Mthatha is 'How can you enjoy eating a sweet while it is covered in paper?' (Church HIV and AIDS worker).

Our fieldwork revealed that the church is struggling to be relevant in this context. Teaching from the evangelical churches comes primarily in the form of negative, unsupportive and blame-laden comments, such as 'you have HIV because of your promiscuity'. The message given out is that 'sex is bad and sex is wrong' (personal communication, NGO worker), with an over-riding emphasis on judgement. It also became clear during our fieldwork that some churches are failing to engage with this situation. They seemed unable or unwilling to help equip young women to withstand the pressures mentioned and despite the fact that young people repeatedly expressed an emotional need for help in dealing with issues of sexual intimacy, churches were not offering this. Churches are failing to provide a safe space where men and women can share their anxieties and work through the changing social context in which they live. Our research showed that the church is not playing the positive role it could in restoring people's sense of self-worth and value.

It is not only in its lack of response to the crisis that the church is struggling. At the same time, it is failing to lead by example on matters of sex, gender relations and HIV and AIDS in its own behaviour. In a society where displays of masculinity are extremely important, men still take most positions of leadership in the church. Some men in these positions are known to abuse their power, for example, by being unfaithful to their wives. As a result there is a considerable, visible collision between what the church preaches and the reality its leaders practise. Rather than living lives that affirm basic Christian beliefs and therefore setting an example to the rest of society, some leaders' practices mirror a society that conflicts with these Christian teachings. As one interviewee said, the church is seen to 'look good on the outside and underneath has a broken and disturbed sense of self and being'.

Burkina Faso and Zimbabwe

There are some similarities between what we found in South Africa and what we found in Burkina Faso and Zimbabwe. For example, many churches were found to accept prevailing values from society, rather than examine their compatibility with biblical teaching; at the same time, they make selective use of biblical texts to reinforce these values. The focus in some local churches appeared to be strongly on evangelism, rather than discipleship. Whilst evangelism concerns itself primarily with proclaiming the gospel of Christ to convert, discipleship stresses the importance of enabling Christians to live out a new life different from that found in society, calling for behaviour change in line with the focus of following Christ.

In the rural communities that we visited, a common pattern emerged of wives being submissive to their husbands, and the men taking biblical texts out of context in order to back up their opinions and justify the way they treated their wives. In these cases, believing strongly in their own interpretation of the text, the men genuinely believed they were right. One pastor in Zimbabwe, for example, told us, 'I expect my wife to bow down before me as I bow down before Christ.' When asked how he reconciled this with a preceding passage in the Bible, which states that all Christians should 'submit to one another' (Ephesians 5: verse 21) and that husbands are called to love their wives 'as Christ loved the church and gave himself up for her' (Ephesians 5: verse 25), he replied 'We find that difficult.' In Burkina Faso we found this approach of selective interpretation of the Bible had dire consequences for relationships. In some cases, husbands felt they were in 'successful' relationships, when they were in fact using and abusing their wives. Women, on the other hand, felt very differently, as one woman's comment sums up: 'Our husbands treat us like beasts and animals. They come in, have sex and leave.'

These sensitive and difficult situations are unlikely to be appreciated by church leaders, who are usually men. In rural Zimbabwe in particular, this is so despite the fact that the adult congregation is almost entirely female. There, even if male leaders do have an understanding for or sympathy with women, they have little standing with men outside the church, who see church as a place for women and children. 'What can I do? The men don't come to church and when I visit homes they don't want to speak to me', said one pastor we spoke to in rural Zimbabwe. In Burkina Faso and urban Zimbabwe, where there are relatively higher proportions of men within congregations, it is more possible to work with couples.

One long-term strategy used in both countries is to improve the training of church leaders and their understanding of biblical teaching on sex and marriage, particularly around the role of sex to bring pleasure to both husband and wife, and deepen their relationship. In Zimbabwe, CAT is already working with a local theological training institute to train new pastors on HIV and AIDS. So many of the congregations now face this issue that it is seen as essential to equip pastors to deal with the reality of the problems they will face.

Conclusion

Underlying inequalities in gender relations exacerbate the impact HIV and AIDS are having on women and girls. Women are often the most vulnerable and marginalized within African communities. Our visits to Mthatha, Pietermaritzburg, Bulawayo, and Ouagadougou confirmed that the church has, at times, misunderstood biblical teaching and, as a result, contributed to the problem. In the absence of teaching to the contrary, church adherents assume that the church endorses traditional values and practices relating to gender. Some evangelical churches maintain traditional values, for instance that women should serve, and be subservient to, men, rather than teaching equal submission in love. This has serious implications in the context of HIV and AIDS. Among other things, married women within the church are unable to challenge the unfaithfulness of their husbands, or negotiate the use of a condom for safer sex. Both these situations may increase the risk of infection with HIV. The church has failed to provide leadership to young people, especially young women, facing huge pressure to be sexually active.

The call to action

On the basis of this research, Tearfund is funding a small pilot initiative to try new ways of working with the church to change behaviours, and to balance biblical theology and work to address the gender inequity in the relationships between men and women in the church. Working with and funding the two partners, Vigilance and CAT, the pilot programme seeks to gain a better understanding of the gender issues in the evangelical church context and facilitate a change in attitudes in the areas where the partners work. Vigilance and CAT will work with a number of churches exploring issues of gender, sexual rights and HIV and AIDS with the intention of enabling them to find appropriate responses to the issues. In doing so, the programme hopes to mobilize men and women to reduce the vulnerability of women and girls to HIV and AIDS. The evangelical churches in Africa are uniquely placed, often at the centre of the community, enjoying respect and exercising influence with a wide-ranging audience and therefore well able to bring about positive change. This uniqueness has not been fully exploited when looking at gender inequity and its relationship to the spread of HIV and AIDS across Africa. The church can be a catalyst for change in the local community, transforming lives, attitudes and behaviour.

The response proposed in Zimbabwe and Burkina Faso is essentially to bring the message of God's intended relationships between men and women to different groups. In Zimbabwe, CAT will emphasize changing the values of a local community, as there is evidence that community norms determine individuals' behaviour. In a high-density urban area, this will take place through a local church, targeting different members of the congregation in different ways with a consistent message. In a rural area, a partnership of agencies will communicate a common set of messages to all the key stakeholder groups including school students, men at work, traditional leaders, and church leaders and members, with each agency having particular targets. In Burkina Faso, Vigilance will work through church structures in urban and rural areas by means of in-depth contact with particular groups.

Already, CAT has developed a paper proposing a position for local churches to agree on gender and HIV and AIDS. This sets out 'supra-cultural' principles for all Christians, asserting that the church should acknowledge that God has made men and women different but equal, and address the implications of this, especially in terms of empowering young women.

If successful, it is expected that the process will be used in other communities, theological institutions and pastoral training courses to influence and transform present and future church leaders. Local people external to the churches, but who understand the context, language and culture of the church in Africa, will facilitate the entire process.

CAT and Vigilance will face their own organizational challenges as they work on this project and will face external opposition in some areas as they move forward. Tearfund believes that prayer is an integral part of all that we do, that God answers prayer and that this can bring about change. Given this belief, the project will include the establishment of a regular prayer group to pray about this specific issue over the next two years, and to ask for help and guidance in the challenges CAT and Vigilance may face.

Future issues

As mentioned before, if these activities are successful, there will be scope to extend the interventions to many other places where African Christian leaders are recognizing the need to address what the church believes and communicates concerning gender relations, especially in the context of HIV and AIDS. This could be the beginning of a movement of leaders in the evangelical church in Africa who are restless with the church and want to work with it to equip it to take on the challenges ahead. The church is a powerful institution which, harnessed for good, can make a massive impact.

There is always hope for the future and a recognition that changes can and do happen. A doctor at the workshop in Zimbabwe looking at the issue of gender, HIV and the church said, 'I have begun to see God using me more even amongst my colleagues at work. I know the workshop didn't just benefit me in terms of ideas but a spiritual deposit was put in my heart that has left me not the same.'

Tearfund hopes this attitude will spread among many Christians across Africa and begin a movement for change that will leave the continent transformed.

Notes

We are grateful to all of the people who, graciously and so generously, gave us their time, thoughts and resources during our field visits. Particular thanks to the staff of Christian AIDS Taskforce and Vigilance for organizing such comprehensive visits. Also to Lynell Bergen and Brian Dyck, Graham and Colleen Beggs, and Janet and David Cunningham for their generous hospitality.

1   The term 'evangelical' comes from the Greek word for 'Gospel' or 'good news'. To be *evangelical* means to be acting in agreement with spreading *the good news* message of the New Testament. The word 'evangelicalism' usually refers to branches of Christianity typified by an emphasis on a personal experience of conversion, biblically oriented faith, and a belief in the relevance of the Christian faith to cultural issues, including social justice.

Evangelicals are found in a wide range of denominations. Many groups in the South are fast growing, especially among poor communities. The size of the evangelical movement inevitably leads to diversity. For example, in North America evangelicalism tends to have an image of being politically and theologically conservative, although many North American evangelicals would reject such a caricature. In the UK and many other parts of the world, evangelicals are often strong supporters of social justice. Tearfund acknowledges that parts of the constituency hold unhelpful perspectives and have not responded well to poverty. Tearfund looks to play a critical role in connecting the capacities and resources of its supporter base in the UK with Christians in the South who are committed to its principles, and in challenging other evangelicals in both the North and South.

2   For background information see: www.tearfund.org

3   Gender in Relief and Development Policy, Tearfund 1998.

4   We define this as men and women being equal in the eyes of God, living in partnership with one another, living together in love, respect, and mutual trust.

5   In many traditions, when a man dies, his family forces his widow either to marry a brother, or at least to sleep with one. The woman has no say in this matter as she is seen as the property of the husband's family. In some areas, this has been ended due to HIV and AIDS, but a brother remains the administrator of all the possessions of the dead man's household. He may then exploit the widow's vulnerability in demanding sexual favours.

6   This is a cultural practice where a girl, or a wife, is given to a male visitor for sexual intercourse as a demonstration of welcome and friendship.

7   In parts of Southern Africa, women believe that men are more sexually satisfied if their vagina is 'dry'. So, they go out of their way to use herbs and other inserted material that cause the vagina to be dry in the belief that men prefer or require this. This makes them more vulnerable to infection.

References

Agadjanian, V. (2005) 'Gender, religious involvement, and HIV/AIDS prevention in Mozambique', *Social Science & Medicine* 61 (2005): 1529–39.

Anglican Communion News Service 'Pastoral letter from the Primates of the Anglican Communion, 27 May 2003'. http://www.anglicancommunion. org/acns/articles/34/50/acns3450.html (last accessed July 2006).

Dilley, V. and Sheerattan-Bisnauth, P. (2003) 'Report: Consultation on Gender and HIV/AIDS. Makurdi, Benue State, Nigeria. 5–11 March 2003'. World Alliance of Reformed Churches, Geneva.

Dube, M. (2003) 'A Vision for Mission in the 21st Century: Ways Ahead for Ecumenical Theological Education: HIV/AIDS and Other Challenges in the New Millennium'. Keynote address at St Paul's United Theological College, Limuru, Kenya, 6 March. http://www.thecirclecawt.org/focus_ areas?mode=content&id=17293&refto=2629 (last accessed July 2006)

Dube, M. and Kanyoro, M. (eds) (2004) *Grant Me Justice: HIV/AIDS and Gender Readings of the Bible,* Cluster Publications, Pietermaritzburg.

Farley, M. (2004) 'Partnership in Hope: Gender, Faith and Responses to HIV/ AIDS in Africa', *Journal of Feminist Studies in Religion*, 20(1): 133–48.

Khathide, A. and Dube, W. (ed) (2003) 'Teaching and talking about our sexuality: a means of combating HIV/AIDS', Chapter 2 in Musa W. Dube (ed.) *HIV/AIDS in the Curriculum: Methods of Integrating HIV/AIDS into Theological Programmes*, WCC, Geneva, http://www.wcccoe.org/wcc/what/mission/ dube-2.html (last accessed 14 April 2011).

Mash, R. and Kareithi, R. (2005) *Fikelela AIDS Project Youth and Sexuality Research. Ages 12-19 years in the Diocese of Cape Town, South Africa*, Fikelela, Cape Town.

Moyo, F. (2002) 'Singing and Dancing Women's Liberation: My Story of Faith'. http://www.pcusa.org/globaled/moyoarticle.htm (last accessed July 2006).

Mwaura, P. (2004) 'Integrity of Mission in the Light of the Gospel: Bearing witness of the Spirit among Africa's Gospel Bearers'. Paper presented at 11th International Conference of the International Association of Mission Studies, Malaysia, 31 July – 7 August 2004. http://www.missionstudies. org/conference/0plenary_papers/Philomena_Mwaura.pdf (last accessed July 2006).

Phiri, I. (2003) 'The Circle's Response to HIV/AIDS'. Excerpts from keynote address, Addis Ababa. http://www.thecirclecawt.org/annual_2003_15 (last accessed July 2006).

Phiri, I. and Masenya, M. (2003) *African Women, HIV/AIDS and Faith Communities*, Cluster Publications, Pietermaritzburg.

Trinitapoli, J. and Regnerus, M. (2005) *Religion and HIV Risk Behaviors among Men: Initial Results from a Panel Study in Rural Sub-Saharan Africa*, Population Research Centre, Austin.

UNAIDS (2006) *Report on the Global AIDS Epidemic*, UNAIDS, Geneva.

UNAIDS, UNFPA and UNIFEM (2004) *'Prevention' in Women and AIDS: Confronting the Crisis*, a joint report by UNAIDS/UNFPA/UNIFEM, Geneva.

World Alliance of Reformed Churches (2003) *Created in God's Image: From Hierarchy to Partnership. A Church Manual for Gender Awareness and Leadership Development*, World Alliance of Reformed Churches, Geneva.

About the authors

Mandy Marshall is Tearfund's Gender Advisor focusing on gender in relief and development. She has worked for Tearfund in a variety of roles and has travelled extensively. Before joining Tearfund Mandy worked in India on a project for girls.

Nigel Taylor is an independent development consultant, with long experience relating to Africa. He is particularly interested in the response to HIV and AIDS, especially enhancing the effectiveness of international aid, and the role of faith, and faith-based organisations. He dedicates this chapter to the memory of Yvonne Dlomo, Natasha Ndlovu, and many other women of Africa who have inspired him, but smile no more because of AIDS.

Chapter 4

The Thai *bhikkhuni* movement and women's empowerment

Emma Tomalin

This chapter first appeared in *Gender & Development* Volume 14, Issue 3, November 2006, p. 385–97

This paper discusses the recent emergence of a movement in Thailand that aims to critique and transform patriarchal values supported by the Theravada Buddhist tradition by introducing female ordination (bhikkhuni ordination). The paper argues that there is a relationship between the low status of women in Thai Buddhism and the inferior status of women in Thai society. The introduction of female leadership roles in Thai Buddhism could play a role in balancing the gender hierarchies within the tradition as well as in society more broadly.

Introduction

In the field of gender and development, an understanding of the influence that religious and cultural traditions have upon women's social status or economic opportunity is slowly being recognized as an important factor in the pursuit of female empowerment in developing countries. While institutional religion can legitimize values and rules that disempower women, the importance of religion in the lives of millions of poor women across the globe means that secular feminism is often perceived not only as Western but also as lacking cultural relevance (Peach 2000).

In response, rather than rejecting religion for its inherent patriarchy, styles of 'religious feminism' have emerged. These argue for re-interpretations of religious systems that are consistent with the 'core' values of the tradition as well as various types of feminist thinking. Such a strategy is attractive to women who wish to employ a religious narrative to guide their politics of empowerment, rather than relying on the secular rhetoric of mainstream (Western) feminist discourses. While we should be sceptical about research which depicts poor, non-Western women as essentially religious, or which reduces gender oppression to religious or cultural causes, an increased sensitivity to the role of religious and cultural factors in shaping gender relations is a welcome shift in development theory and practice.

A key challenge, however, faces 'religious feminists', since women rarely occupy the positions of status and authority in religious traditions that would enable them to challenge misogynistic tendencies. The aim of this paper is to discuss the recent emergence of a movement in Thailand that aims to critique and transform patriarchal values supported by the Theravada Buddhist[1] tradition through introducing the ordination of women into religious orders, or the *bhikkhuni* ordination.[2] A strong theme within this movement is the argument that gender hierarchies in Thai Buddhism have a broader cultural impact on social attitudes that disempower women. Many advocates of the *bhikkhuni* ordination consider that there is a very direct relationship between the low status of women in Thai Buddhism and the inferior status of women in Thai society, which places them at risk of abuses such as domestic violence and sex trafficking, as well an increased vulnerability to HIV. For instance, as the activist and writer Khuankaew suggests:

> One of the core causes of violence against women has not yet been touched upon – the beliefs, attitudes, traditions, and values that come out of a patriarchal society influenced by Buddhism itself ... in the discussions at the local, national and international meetings of women organizations the root causes of prostitution have always been poverty, western models of development and modernization ... Hardly mentioned as a cause of prostitution is the lack of leadership roles for women in Buddhism. (2002: 16)

In this paper I will first discuss the position of women in Thai Buddhism and the significance of the *bhikkhuni* ordination. The introduction of the *bhikkhuni* ordination into Thailand is considered to be significant not only for religious reasons, benefiting women who choose to embark on this religious life and the renouncement of many material comforts that accompanies it, but also for its potential to be empowering to women more broadly. I will then move on to discuss some of the academic literature that examines the relationship between Thai Buddhism and women's oppression in Thailand, particularly with respect to the issues of sex trafficking and HIV (Thitsa 1980; Peach 2000, 2005; Klunklin and Greenwood 2005). Finally, I will examine the recent emergence of the Thai *bhikkhuni* movement as a 'local strategy' to address gender inequalities within the social system.

The history and significance of the *bhikkhuni* ordination movement in Thailand

While the Buddhist texts tell us that the Buddha established a male religious order (*bhikkhu sangha*)[3] as well as a female religious order (*bhikkhuni sangha*), there is no historical evidence that the *bhikkhuni* tradition was actually established in Thailand (Kabilsingh 1991; Owen 1998). Sri Lanka, India and Burma are the only countries where Theravada *bhikkhunis* ever existed, and by the eleventh century CE they had disappeared completely from Theravada

Buddhism. By contrast, in the Mahayana tradition the *bhikkhuni* order exists to this day. In Thailand the only formal religious option available to women is life as a white robed *mae chi*. The *mae chi* institution is not mentioned in the texts, in fact its exact origins are unclear (Lindberg-Falk 2000: 45), and many view it as a poor substitute for the *bhikkhuni* ideal. The living conditions of a *mae chi* are often inadequate, they have little opportunity for study of the *dhamma* (Buddhist teachings), and the majority live in temples, where they cook and clean for the monks (Mueke 2004). Whereas lay Buddhists give generously to the monks, since they represent authentic 'fields of merit',[4] donations to a *mae chi* generate less merit and therefore people give less generously. Like *bhikkhunis*, women who become *mae chis* shave their heads and eyebrows, give up their possessions and practise celibacy. However, they only follow eight, or sometimes ten, precepts rather than the 311 rules of the *bhikkhuni patimokkha*.[5] This would seem to place them closer to lay Buddhists, who observe five precepts. The low status of the *mae chi* is further compounded by the ambiguous way in which they are dealt with by different government ministries in Thailand: there is no consensus about whether they are actually religious or lay persons. While the Ministry of the Interior defines the *mae chi* as a 'skilled ordinand' (candidate for ordination) who has renounced worldly concerns and, like monks, not eligible to vote, both the Department of Religion and the Ministry of Communications treat them as lay women. Thus, the Department of Religion underwrites education for monks and novices but not for *mae chis,* and the Ministry of Communications grants travel subsidies to monks but not to *mae chis* (Lindberg-Falk 2000, 42; Mueke 2004: 225).

It has proved difficult to revive the *bhikkhuni* ordination in Theravada Buddhism, since the conventional ordination procedure necessitates the presence of at least five male and five female ordinands (the 'dual ordination'). One possible approach to this apparent deadlock has been the recognition that, although the Buddhist literature tells us that the dual ordination is the ideal, it does not declare other forms of ordination invalid (Bhadra 2002). For instance, the first Buddhist nun, Mahapajapati, was ordained by receiving eight special rules, *garudhammas*, from the Buddha, and in Sri Lanka, before the arrival of *bhikkhunis* from India in the third century BCE, it is recorded that male *bhikkhus* alone were permitted to ordain women (Li 2000: 183). This departure from the conventional ordination procedure has not, however, been the strategy employed to revive the ordination, firstly in the USA (1988), then in India (1996), and Sri Lanka (1998). Instead, the dual ordination has been retained, but the required number of *bhikkhunis* has been achieved through the presence of nuns from the Chinese Dharmaguptaka tradition of Mahayana Buddhism. While many reject this for not being an authentic Theravada ordination, others argue that it is legitimate since it was a group of *bhikkhunis* from Sri Lanka who introduced the *bhikkhuni* ordination into China in 433 CE. The Sri Lankan and Chinese *bhikkhunis*, therefore, share the same lineage (Kabilsingh 1991: 31; Wijayasundara 2000: 82).

The revival of the *bhikkhuni* tradition in Sri Lanka in 1998 was a major mile-stone, since 70 per cent[6] of Sri Lankans are Buddhist, whereas Buddhism accounts for only 0.8 per cent[7] of the population of India and much less in the USA. Although in Sri Lanka there are opponents of the *bhikkhuni* ordination, and it has not been officially recognized by the 'Maha Sangha'[8] (Lee and Bhadra 2002: 33), a number of high profile monks have given their support and the response of the lay community has been generally positive. It is estimated that there are around four hundred *bhikkhunis* in Sri Lanka. The situation is somewhat different in Thailand, where to date only five Thai women live as Theravada *bhikkhunis,* and where monks are specifically banned from ordaining women under the 1928 Sangha Act.[9] Neither the public nor the monastic community, or *sangha,* have been particularly welcoming towards the introduction of the *bhikkhuni* tradition in Thailand. There is a fairly broad consensus in Thailand that women's status and options within Buddhism need to undergo reform, but many argue that it is more appropriate to work towards transforming the *mae chi* institution rather than to introduce the *bhikkhuni* ordination. Lindberg-Falk suggests that the *mae chi* institution is already undergoing a process of reform, particularly through the emergence of 'independent nunneries' where women have the opportunity for education and religious practice (2000). Moreover, the 'Mae Chi Institute' (established in 1969) is behind a campaign for legal change that would recognize *mae chis* as authentic religious persons and grant them the same rights as *bhikkhus.*[10] In fact, Lindberg-Falk tells us that the majority of nuns she has interviewed would not want to become *bhikkhunis.* Many of them see it as part of the Mahayana tradition or would be daunted by having to follow all the 311 *bhikkhuni* precepts. Furthermore, the benefits of remaining 'independent' and apart from the male *sangha* could avoid 'institutionalized subordination to the monks' (Lindberg-Falk 2000: 55).

Others, however, are dismissive of this reasoning and instead stress that the introduction of the *bhikkhuni* ordination is congruent with the 'true inten-tions' of the Buddha to establish the 'four-fold *sangha*' consisting of *bhikkhus, bhikkhunis,* lay men (*upasaka*) and lay women (*upasika*) (Wijayasundara 2000).[11] In addition to this religious reason, many also draw attention to the social dimension of women's exclusion from full ordination in Thailand. They argue that the revival of the *bhikkhuni* ordination in Thailand is an impor-tant step in improving women's social status and opportunities more broadly (Ekachai 2001; Kabilsingh 1991; Satha-Anand 1999). In the next section I will explore the theory behind the link between the *bhikkhuni* ordination and women's empowerment.

The theory behind the link between the *bhikkhuni* ordination and women's empowerment

The link between the *bhikkhuni* ordination and women's empowerment has been discussed in academic literature (e.g. Puntarigvivat 2001; Satha-Anand 1999), as well as by people I have interviewed in Thailand (both lay and ordained). There is concern that many gender-related issues facing women in Thailand, including domestic violence, sex trafficking and HIV transmission, have a religious and cultural dimension that is frequently overlooked by secular development agencies, as well as by the Buddhist establishment. Two main themes have emerged in my discussions with ordained and lay Buddhist women in Thailand concerning the social benefits of the *bhikkhuni* ordination. The first theme draws attention to the practical role of Buddhism in providing various services to the community. While many young boys spend time living in temples as temporary monks, where they receive a free religious and general education, this opportunity is denied to girls. This, it is argued, exacerbates the likelihood of the sex trafficking of young girls. The boys who become 'temporary monks' come from socially deprived backgrounds, and girls from similar backgrounds are those who are most likely to end up trafficked into the sex trade. The opportunity to become 'temporary nuns' would, it is argued, help prevent this from happening. The creation of a respected and recognized community of female ordinands in Thai Buddhism would enable the institutionalization of education in the temples for girls as well as boys. Moreover, it is envisioned that female ordinands would be able to offer an informal counselling service to women who have suffered abuse or problems with their marriages, or have contracted HIV. The *bhikkhus* are typically consulted by lay Buddhists for advice and support, but cultural constraints make it difficult for women to seek spiritual and practical advice from male religious persons, particularly regarding issues of a sexual nature.

The second theme raised by those I interviewed concerns the perception that the subordinate status of women in Thai Buddhism has a negative influence on social attitudes about gender roles more broadly (Rattanavali and Earth 2003). This is also reflected in academic literature concerned with gender and Buddhism. As Van Esterik writes, Buddhism is a 'key component of Thai identity' providing 'a way of viewing the world, a sense of reality, moral standards, and a shared language and metaphors for analyzing their existing life situation' (2000: 65-66; Peach 2005: 124). Buddhism reinforces the understanding that women are a lower rebirth than men because of *kamma* acquired in previous lives (Owen 1998) and 'women are socialized to be relational, socially embedded and family oriented rather than independent, autonomous, self-determining individuals' (Peach 2005, 124). This intrinsic inferiority of women is reinforced within the structure of everyday public Buddhist practice and custom:

> Men perform all the public roles of Buddhism, ordained as monks or as lay officiants, leading the chanting, conducting rituals, and participating as members of the *wat* (temple) committee. In addition, the organization of space in the meeting hall clearly denotes the differential status distinctions between monks and lay persons, elders and younger people, and women and men. Monks sit upon a raised platform, denoting higher status. Elderly men sit closest to the monks, followed by younger men. Women sit around the perimeter. The elderly men make merit by placing food in the monks' bowls first, followed by the younger men. Not until the

youngest boy has made his offering will the most elderly woman lead the other women to make their offerings. (Klunklin and Greenwood 2005: 48)

Thus, in the course of my research, it has become clear that an important dimension of the *bhikkhuni* ordination in Thailand is its potential to rebalance this institutionalized hierarchy, which is very much part of Buddhism but also of Thai society more broadly. While not all *bhikkhunis* or aspiring ordinands are explicitly motivated by such a 'feminist' agenda, it is anticipated that the introduction of the *bhikkhuni* ordination may have the effect of transforming attitudes, which would benefit women more broadly. As Puntarigvivat argues 'the replacement of *mae chi* by a *bhikkhuni* institution would greatly raise women's status at the core of Thai culture and would begin to address many of women's problems in Thailand – including poverty, child abuse and prostitution' (2001: 225). Before I go on to discuss the emergent *bhikkhuni* movement in Thailand, I will first review some of the recent literature that discusses the relationship between Thai Buddhism, gender, and women's oppression. These studies particularly focus on links between Buddhism, sex trafficking and women's vulnerability to HIV, and they reflect the concerns of many of the lay and ordained women that I have interviewed in Thailand. The following discussion will provide some important examples of the suggested effects of traditional Buddhist patriarchal views which the *bhikkhuni* movement is attempting to address.

Thai Buddhism and gender: HIV and sex trafficking

The problem of HIV and AIDS is one of the most pressing issues facing developing countries. While the pandemic is most acute in sub-Saharan Africa, southeast Asia, including Thailand, has also been hit hard. In all these regions it is often women who have been worst affected, due to both their physiology and the cultural and social norms that make it difficult for them to ensure safe sexual activity. Klunklin and Greenwood's study of the relationship between Buddhism and the spread of HIV in Thailand argues that 'Thai culture, particularly Buddhism, folklore, and ancient superstitions, affects gender roles and ... the incidence and rapid spread of HIV/AIDS in Thai women' (2005: 46). The superior status of men in the Buddhist tradition and the belief in women's 'kammic deficit' finds further reinforcement, they argue, in notions of the ideal Thai woman (*kunlasatri*) as 'proficient and sophisticated in household duties; graceful and pleasant yet unassuming in appearance and social manners; and conservative in her sexuality' (2005: 49). Central to an understanding of the ideal *kunlasatri* is the notion of *krengjai*, social rules and protocols learnt from childhood that ensure familial and social harmony. However, these are hierarchical and gendered, stressing the subservience of women to their male partners, such that the *kunlasatri* is 'expected to trust and believe in her partner's honesty and fidelity even when she has evidence to the contrary' (Klunklin and Greenwood 2005: 52). Thus, to insist on condom use in a marital relationship can be perceived as not trusting one's husband or as evidence of one's own infidelity.

While the *kunlasatri* ideal is arguably one factor in increasing women's vulnerability to HIV, this is exacerbated by the high proportion of men who have sex with prostitutes after marriage. Buddhism does not condone prostitution, but the *sangha* in Thailand has been criticized for not taking a clear stance on the issue. Some suggest that this would harm the interests of the *sangha*, since the monks receive substantial monetary donations from commercial sex workers (Mueke 1992; Peach 2000, 2005). Others, by contrast, point out that prostitution 'is not considered to be a sin in Buddhism as it is in Christianity, Islam, or other religions, and prostitutes are not always viewed negatively in Buddhist teachings' (Peach 2000: 70–1). Therefore, the *sangha* is less compelled to take a stance on commercial sex work as an ethical issue. However, many are calling on the *sangha* to apply Buddhist ethical teachings to the issue of sex trafficking, invoking the precepts of non-harm (*ahimsa*) and avoidance of sexual misconduct,[12] or stressing that prostitution leads to the accumulation of 'negative karma by reinforcing craving and attachment to the sensual world of desire (which perpetuates bondage to *samsara*)' (Peach 2000: 70).[13]

Girls and women enter prostitution in Thailand for complex reasons, and researchers are likely to point to the lack of educational and economic opportunities for poor females, as well as the demands of a profitable sex-tourism industry. However, a number of studies have suggested that cultural factors also play a part in sustaining the sex industry in Thailand. The tendency of Buddhist teachings not to view sex work as immoral or degrading removes much of the stigma associated with similar work in many other cultures (Peach 2005: 125): In Thai culture prostitutes are not viewed with universal negativity and in the Buddhist texts we find stories about prostitutes, often as friends of the Buddha. Moreover, as Peach tells us, one popular attitude towards prostitution in Thailand is that it enables women to earn money that they can give as donations to monks. This provides them with an opportunity to earn merit in order to improve their *kamma* for a better rebirth in the next life (i.e. as a man) (2005: 125). Thus, 'traditional Thai Buddhist culture functions to legitimate the trafficking industry, and thereby deny the human rights of women involved in sexual slavery' (Peach 2000: 65; Mueke 1992; Puntarigvivat 2001: 227; Kabilsingh 1991: 67; Satha-Anand 1999).

Although this understanding of *kamma* is embedded in Thai society, the Buddhist tradition can also be interpreted to support the view that men and women are equal; it can thus provide 'sources of empowerment and liberation for women' (Peach 2000: 81). This feminist exposition of Buddhism has become the subject of numerous books and articles in different Buddhist traditions. These studies emphasize men and women's equal ability to gain enlightenment (Murcott 1991; Sponberg 1992), positive images of women and the feminine in the texts (Murcott 1991; Peach 2000), as well as the existence of the *bhikkhuni* ordination at the time of the Buddha (Owen 1998). For instance, one popular view is that Buddhist teachings are essentially gender neutral and any patriarchal influences are later corruptions of the tradition. However, are such feminist interpretations of the Buddhist texts relevant in practice? Or do they represent elite perspectives that have emerged within a context of Western feminist critique and have little relevance at the grassroots level? For instance, reading the work of some Buddhist feminist authors one gets the impression that they are speaking about a generic Buddhism that has been responsive to gender issues and concerns as it has translocated to the West, rather than Buddhism as it is actually lived and practised in Asian contexts (see, for instance, Gross 1993). As Peach writes:

> Who is doing the reinterpreting, and for what audience? Would the reinterpreted texts be taught in school? If not, how would the reinterpretations be disseminated? Do Thai women – especially mothers and prostitutes – read Buddhist texts? If not, is it reasonable to assume that Buddhist monks will recite reinterpreted scriptures in religious services? What other mechanisms are available within local communities to communicate these new understandings to women? More generally, it may not always be possible to empower women using a 'local' cultural strategy such as textual reinterpretation, in part because of explicit religious or cultural restrictions on women's autonomy to engage in such practices, including women's basic literacy skills. (2000: 80)

If 'religious feminism' is to be a facilitator of women's empowerment at the grassroots level, then it is necessary to find ways of bridging the gap between feminist interpretations of the tradition and the oppressive dimensions of Thai Buddhism in practice. The final section of this paper discusses recent attempts to introduce the *bhikkhuni* ordination into Thai Buddhism. This is seen as a 'local cultural strategy', to challenge and transform aspects of the tradition which are gender-biased against women and which feed into broader social attitudes that increase women's vulnerability to risks such as domestic violence, sex trafficking or HIV.

The Thai *bhikkhuni* movement and women's empowerment

Since 2002 I have been closely following the progress of the Thai *bhikkhuni* movement via email, letters and visits to Thailand. While so far there has been no formal indication that the 'Supreme Sangha Council' intends to recognize and support the *bhikkhuni* ordination in Thailand, or that the 1928 Sangha Act banning monks from ordaining women will be repealed, its renaissance in Sri Lanka has set a precedent, many hope, for its eventual acceptance in Thailand. Others are more conservative (or pessimistic) and doubt that it will ever become an official institution within the Buddhist tradition in Thailand. However, rather than waiting for the go-ahead from the male religious establishment, a small number of Thai women have now been ordained 'unofficially' as *bhikkhunis*. In 2003 the first Thai *bhikkhuni* was ordained in Sri Lanka[14] and since then a further twenty or so women have been ordained as *samaneris*, or novices. While most of these women have travelled to Sri Lanka for their *samaneri* ordination, I am aware of one monk who is prepared to go against convention and ordain female novices. In February 2006 one of these *samaneris* was ordained in Thailand as a *bhikkhuni* in an ordination that involved only *bhikkhus,* and in March 2006 a further three novices were ordained in the presence of Mahayana nuns (from Taiwan) and Theravada monks. These ordinations are not recognized by the Thai *sangha* and were performed in the open air in the ancient Buddhist ruins at Ayuthaya, around 50 km from Bangkok, rather than at an established Buddhist temple. While the reintroduction of the *bhikkhuni* tradition in Sri Lanka has been crucial to its emergence in Thailand, travel to Sri Lanka is too expensive for poor women who may wish to be ordained. Although the first Thai woman to be ordained as a *bhikkhuni* was a university professor, this is not the typical profile of an aspiring *bhikkhuni* in Thailand. Many have spent years living as *mae chis*; they do not come from economically affluent backgrounds and only some have formal education. Thus, the ordination of women on Thai soil is important if the tradition is to take off.

Despite such developments, a number of the women I have spoken to have told me that once they took on the orange robes (following their ordination as either a *samaneri* or a *bhikkhuni*) they have, at the very least, attracted unwanted attention and, at the very worst, been subjected to harassment and police questioning. The orange-robed monk has a deep symbolic association in Thailand with masculinity. Indeed, in Thai society generally, there is a perception that the practice of women wearing the orange robes is an attempt to make 'women like men' and hence the *bhikkhuni* movement can fall foul of the critique that it is a 'Western feminist imposition'. Nevertheless, the movement considers that the taking on of orange robes by nuns is grounded in an authentic reading of the Buddhist tradition as requiring the 'four-fold *sangha*', even if this breaks with the (patriarchal) customs of Thai Buddhism. Apart from negative social opinion, on a more practical level once a woman decides to become ordained as a novice and to wear the orange robes, then it is likely that she can no longer remain in the temple that has been her home as a *mae chi* (because her ordination is not considered to be authentic to the Theravada tradition). This increases women's vulnerability as they embark on the path to becoming fully ordained. Thus, the conditions for many *mae chis* may be less than desirable, but they are provided with a level of security that many women would be unwilling to forgo.

Although the numbers of *samaneris* and *bhikkhunis* in Thailand are currently very low, there is some indication that negative social attitudes are becoming less pronounced, and the people I spoke to are hopeful that this will encourage more women to embark upon this religious path. Perhaps another obstacle to be overcome, however, is the fact that the emergent '*bhikkhuni* movement' constitutes a loose network of women, rather than a formal organization with a base and leader. The *samaneris* and *bhikkhunis* have not coalesced around a particular temple/nunnery or teacher: they do not reside together in a religious community, but are dispersed throughout Thailand living off alms and donations. They are, however, linked to broader networks of Buddhist women in both Thailand and abroad. In Thailand there is a network of lay

Buddhists, *bhikkhunis* from Mahayana countries, *mae chis* and Western female ordinands,[15] who provide support (both financial and moral) to the Thai *bhikkhunis*. On an international level, the Thai *bhikkhuni* movement reflects a broader campaign to secure equal ordination rights and status for women across Buddhist traditions. There are a number of 'international' events that enable information exchange between women from different traditions. The first of these is the annual awards ceremony for 'Outstanding Women in Buddhism' that has been held since 2002 on International Women's Day at the United Nations in Bangkok. The second is the biennial conference of the Buddhist women's organization Sakyadhita. Both these events involve the participation of Buddhist women and academics from different traditions and countries, to share ideas and to celebrate achievements.

Conclusion

It has not been my intention in this paper to judge the authenticity of the *bhikkhuni* movement either in theory or in practice. Nor have I critically assessed the arguments that link women's oppression in Thailand to features of Buddhist culture. Rather my interest is to highlight the discourses used within the *bhikkhuni* movement as a local religious feminist strategy which aims to challenge and transform the social attitudes that lead to various types of gender-based oppression. I have presented a case study that indicates the potential usefulness of the nurturing of female leadership roles within religious traditions which are socially powerful, on the one hand, and patriarchal on the other. While it is unlikely that the feminist transformation of religious traditions alone is capable of mitigating women's oppression across the globe, in conjunction with other technical, political, or legal strategies it presents a potentially fruitful, yet largely overlooked, dimension of women's empowerment.

Notes

1   Buddhism is usually divided into three main types: Theravada Buddhism (practised today in Thailand, Sri Lanka, Myanmar/Burma, Cambodia, and Laos), Mahayana Buddhism (practised today in Vietnam, China, Japan and Korea) and Vajrayana/Tibetan Buddhism. See Skilton (1994) for a discussion of the history and doctrines of each tradition.

2   Since 2002 I have been closely following the developing Thai *bhikkhuni* movement. This research has been funded by a British Academy small grant.

3   In the Buddhist tradition the *sangha* is part of the so-called 'triple gem' or 'three refuges' consisting of the Buddha, the *dharma* (the Buddha's teachings) and the *sangha* (the Buddhist monastic community). These are the three things that Buddhists give themselves to or 'take refuge in'.

4   Giving food alms and donations both to monks (*bhikkhus*) and to fully ordained nuns (*bhikkhunis*) is believed to confer religious merit on the

donors, which increases their positive *kamma* and improves their chances of a favourable rebirth. Most merit is accumulated through giving to monks, and as such they are considered to be authentic 'fields of merit'. *Mae chis*, however, are not considered to be such 'fields of merit'.

5 By contrast, Theravada *bhikkhus* (monks) have 227 rules (the *bhikkhu patimokkha*). The fact that nuns are expected to keep more rules than monks has received much attention in the literature. Some suggest that that it is a reflection of the Buddha's initial reluctance to allow women to ordain (it is reported that he was asked three times before he agreed) and that the extra rules for nuns effectively make them subservient to the monks (see Owen 1998: 20–6). Others are less convinced that they are discriminatory (i.e. believe they serve to protect rather than control women) or suggest that they were later additions to the tradition and did not reflect the Buddha's intentions (Kabilsingh 1991: 29–30; Tsomo 2000: 27; Kusuma 2000: 20).

6 Data from http://www.adherents.com/largecom/com_buddhist.html (last accessed May 2006).

7 Data from the 2001 Indian census www.censusindia.net/religiondata/Summary%20Buddhists.pdf (last accessed April 2006).

8 The Maha Sangha ('Great Assembly') in Sri Lanka is an elite circle of Buddhist clergy who have influence over important decisions made within the tradition.

9 See Kabilsingh (1991: 45ff) for a discussion of the background to this rule. Although the rule still stands and governs practice, it is actually unconstitutional, since the 1997 National Constitution grants equality to men and women.

10 This call for legal reform was originally heralded by the feminist lawyer Mae Chi Khunying Kanitha Wichiencharoen, now deceased. She was also a pioneer in the broader reform of the *mae chi* institution, establishing the first and only college for post-high-school education for *mae chis*, Mahapajapati Theri College in Khorat. She was the co-founder of the Association for the Promotion of the Status of Women, which runs a shelter for abused women and children in Bangkok.

11 The suggestion that the Buddha's original intention was to establish the 'four-fold *sangha*' seems to be in conflict with his apparent initial reluctance to ordain women (see note 5). However, this is consistent with the broader tendency for religious texts to be open to interpretation from different perspectives and thus supportive of a range of socio-political agendas. For a detailed discussion of the reasons why the Buddha seemed to be reluctant to ordain women, and whether or not this indicates a genuine concern that women are not really capable of leading a renunciate life, see Owen (1998).

12 These are two of the five precepts to which all Buddhists aspire to adhere.

13 *Samsara* is the Buddhist term for the cycle of phenomenal existences into which individuals are repeatedly born. It is the aim of Buddhist practice to obtain release from *samsara* and no longer be reborn.

14 Dhammananda, as she is now known, was previously called Chatsumarn Kabilsingh. She had been married and spent her career as an academic and campaigner for women's ordination. She runs a temple that was

established by her mother (who was ordained as a Taiwanese/Mahayana *bhikkhuni*), the Songdhammakalyani Temple ('the temple of women who uphold *dhamma*'), about 50 km from Bangkok. See the Thaibhikkunis.org website (last accessed April 2006).

15 My initial introduction to the Thai *bhikkhuni* movement was through meeting an ordained Buddhist woman from the USA, who now lives in Thailand as a Theravada *bhikkhuni*. She is an ardent campaigner for female ordination and has supported a number of Thai women who aspire to become ordained.

References

Bhadra, Bhikkhuni (2002) 'Higher ordination that leads to the eradication of defilements'. *World Fellowship of Buddhists Review* 34(3–4).

Ekachai, Sanitsuda (with Nick Wilgus ed.) (2001) *Keeping the Faith: Thai Buddhism at the Crossroads*, Post Publishing, Bangkok.

Gross, R. M. (1993) *Buddhism After Patriarchy: A Feminist History, Analysis, and Reconstruction of Buddhism*, State University of New York Press, Albany.

Kabilsingh, C. (1991) *Thai Women in Buddhism*, Parallax Press, Berkeley.

Khuankaew, O. (2002) 'Buddhism and domestic violence'. *World Fellowship of Buddhists Review* 34(3–4).

Klunklin, A. and Greenwood, J. (2005) 'Buddhism, the status of women and the spread of HIV/AIDS in Thailand'. *Health Care International for Women* 26(1).

Kusuma, Bhikkhuni (2000) 'Inaccuracies in Buddhist women's history'. In Tsomo, K. L. (ed) *Innovative Buddhist Women: Swimming against the Stream* Routledge Curzon, Richmond.

Lee, Bhikkhuni and Bhadra, Bhikkhuni (2002) 'Sri Lankan Buddhist history'. *The World Fellowship of Buddhists Review* 39(3–4): 32–4.

Li, Y. (2000) 'Ordination, legitimacy, and sisterhood: the international full ordination ceremony in Bodhgaya'. In Tsomo, K. L. (ed) *Innovative Buddhist Women: Swimming against the Stream*, Routledge Curzon, Richmond.

Lindberg-Falk, M. (2000) 'Women in between: becoming religious persons in Thailand'. In Findly, E. B. (ed) *Women's Buddhism, Buddhism's Women*, Wisdom Publications, Boston.

Mueke, M.A. (1992) 'Mother sold food, daughter sells her body – the cultural continuity of prostitution'. *Social Science and Medicine* 35(7).

Mueke, M.A. (2004) 'Female sexuality in Thai discourses about Maechii ("lay nuns")'. *Culture, Health and Sexuality* 6(3): 221–38.

Murcott, S. (1991) *The First Buddhist Women: Translations and Commentaries on the Therigatha*, Parallax Press, Berkeley, Calif.

Owen, L. B. (1998) 'On gendered discourse and the maintenance of boundaries: a feminist analysis of the Bhikkhuni Order in Indian Buddhism'. *Asian Journal of Women's Studies* 4(3).

Peach, L. J. (2000) 'Human rights, religion and (sexual) slavery'. *Annual of the Society of Christian Ethics* 20.

Peach, L.J. (2005) '"Sex slaves" or "sex workers"? Cross-cultural and comparative religious perspectives on sexuality, subjectivity, and moral identity in anti-sex trafficking discourse'. *Culture and Religion* 6(1).

Puntarigvivat, T. (2001) 'A Thai Buddhist perspective'. In Raines, J.C. and Maguire, D.C. (eds) *What Men Owe to Women: Men's Voices from World Religions*, State University of New York Press, New York .

Rattanavali, Venerable and Earth, B. (2003) 'Southeast Asia: the socio-religious roots of violence against women in Thailand'. *The World Fellowship of Buddhists Review* 40(3): 33–9.

Satha-Anand, S. (1999) 'Looking to Buddhism to turn back prostitution in Thailand'. In Bauer, J.R. and Bell, D.A. (eds) *The East Asian Challenge for Human Rights*, Cambridge University Press, Cambridge.

Skilton, A. (1994) *A Concise History of Buddhism,* Windhorse Publications, Birmingham.

Sponberg, A. and Cabezon, J. I. (eds) (1992) 'Attitudes toward women and the feminine in early Buddhism'. *Buddhism, Sexuality and Gender*, State University of New York Press, Albany.

Thitsa, K. (1980) *Providence and Prostitution: Image and Reality for Women in Buddhist Thailand,* Change International Reports, London.

Tsomo, K.L. (2000) 'Mahaprajapati's Legacy: the Buddhist women's movement – an introduction'. In Tsomo, K.L. (ed) *Buddhist Women Across Cultures: Realizations,* State University of New York Press, Albany.

Van Esterik, P. (2000) *Materializing Thailand*, Berg Books, Oxford.

Wijayasundara, S. (2000) 'Restoring the order of nuns to the Theravadin tradition'. In Tsomo, K.L. (ed) *Buddhist Women Across Cultures: Realizations*, State University of New York Press, Albany

About the author

Emma Tomalin is Senior Lecturer, in the Department of Theology and Religious Studies, at the University of Leeds

Chapter 5

Reflecting on gender equality in Muslim contexts in Oxfam GB

Adrienne Hopkins and Kirit Patel

This chapter first appeared in *Gender & Development* Volume 14, Issue 3, November 2006, p. 423–35

Gender inequality, faith and development are intrinsically linked, and the impact of religious beliefs and practices on gender inequality is an issue that cannot be ignored in development work. This chapter summarizes the key discussions and findings of two workshops, held by Oxfam GB, on the challenges of working on gender equality issues in Muslim contexts. It explores some of the strategies Oxfam staff have used in their programmes, and highlights the challenges Oxfam will need to address as it develops this area of work further.

Introduction

In the early years of the 21st century, there has been an increasing emphasis on religious and cultural identities as a means of political mobilization. This phenomenon, known as 'identity politics', has significantly altered the global and local arenas of development work, especially relating to gender.

The historical and political landscape of the last decade has done much to shape this phenomenon, mobilizing people of differing faiths and political groups in many parts of the globe. The 'war on terror', and the 'Western' media's failure to distinguish between differing Islamic political and religious groups, have helped to make many Muslims feel increasingly isolated and defensive, and have led to increased polarization within Muslim society. The consequence of these forces has made work dealing with gender equality issues in religious contexts more complex and problematic.

Oxfam recognizes, however, that gender inequality, faith and development are intrinsically linked, meaning that this is an issue we must engage with, no matter how difficult it may be to do so. As a step towards this, Oxfam GB held two workshops (in 2004 and 2006) with a wide range of staff, the majority of whom were themselves Muslim, to explore the challenges faced in working on gender equality in Muslim contexts, and to share learning on practical development interventions and responses at programme level.

This chapter does not represent a thorough analysis of all the issues relating to gender equality in Muslim contexts. Rather, it shares the thoughts and experiences of the workshop participants, explores the challenges they are facing and presents their ideas of possible ways forward for Oxfam's work in this area.

Creating a space for discussion

The first workshop, in May 2004, brought together 20 Oxfam GB staff members and facilitators – 18 women and two men – from 12 countries. Its aims were to provide a structured space for participants to explore the concept of 'Muslim contexts', to identify commonalities and differences in their experiences of working on gender equality, and to understand the impact of religious, political, and other identities on gender equality. It also offered participants the opportunity to increase their confidence in analysing the complex global phenomena that affect them and their work, and to identify and exchange strategies to maintain and enlarge the space to promote gender equality.

Commonalities and differences

A number of important points emerged from the workshop. One of the over-riding conclusions was that participants felt that there was a commonality in the challenges that they were facing, and that an exchange of ideas and experi-ences would be fruitful. However, at the same time, it was recognized that gender inequality exists across all religions and societies, and is not unique to Muslim contexts, and indeed that there is huge diversity across Muslim contexts. In Islam, as in other faiths, religion is an important aspect of identity. It is often used to justify cultural practices, and has been politicized in ways that affect local development. However, participants also highlighted that it is important to recognize that religion is just one aspect of identity, and to recognize the diversity within 'Muslim' groups. It was telling, for example, that participants could not come to agreement on what it is to be 'Muslim'. This served to underline that, above all, Oxfam needs to avoid stereotyping, as this has a huge negative impact on women's rights: the homogenization of diverse groups ignores the diversity of experiences, and often means that women lose their voice in the process. The tendency to portray 'Muslim women' as powerless victims of religiously justified oppression is simplistic, and ignores women's agency. For example, the 'Western' media's typical portrayal of women in Afghanistan as *burqa*-clad and restricted to the home ignores the fact that 'Afghan women have kept up a determined struggle for equality, even during the years of the very oppressive Taliban regime' (Freshta Sayed, Oxfam GB's Gender Adviser in Afghanistan).

Another key point that came out of the workshop was the need for devel-opment practitioners to engage with religion. This is a contentious issue, and development workers may be tempted to shy away from addressing it, but participants underlined the fact that religion cannot be ignored in development work. Oxfam GB's work in Yemen on marriage at an early age shows clearly how gender inequality and religious beliefs interact to perpetuate poverty.

Box 5.1 Campaigning on marriage at an early age in Yemen

More than 50 per cent of girls in Yemen get married before the age of 18. Oxfam and its partners are concerned that marriage of girls under 18 is perpetuating a cycle of poverty.

'I wouldn't wish any girl to go through what I have faced, and I won't allow my little girls to be married as young I was', says Shafika,[1] who got married when she was 13 years old.

It is not uncommon for girls in Yemen to find themselves married as soon as they reach puberty. Young girls become wives and mothers without having the chance to grow up themselves. As a result, they suffer from health risks caused by early sexual relations, pregnancy, and childbirth.

'I first got pregnant when I was 14 years old', says 22-year-old Shafika, now a mother of six. 'In every pregnancy, I faced complications during the birth, and my children and I suffer from ongoing malnutrition.'

Shafika is one of the women that Oxfam's partner organizations met during research in Hodiedah Governorate in western Yemen. Our studies have found that marriage at an early age damages girls' education, health, and skills development, and holds communities back in the struggle to overcome poverty.

As well as causing high maternal and child mortality rates, marriage at an early age means that girls miss out on their education, which in turn affects women's ability to promote their own children's health and education. Shafika's parents took her out of school in the fifth grade so she could get married. Her husband dropped out of school at the same time, and he now makes a precarious daily living by selling vegetables.

So why do so many families choose marriage at an early age for their children? 'My father agreed with his friend that I would marry his son, to take the burden of my keep off my family', says Shafika. Many parents consider daughters to be a drain on the family income. With 41 per cent of the population living below the poverty line, the economic situation is sometimes a contributing factor, but this practice is also driven by deeply ingrained cultural beliefs and religious interpretations.

Local communities are eager to promote intermarriage because it strengthens kinship ties between families. People often don't realize the harm done to the girls and to the communities.

In response, Oxfam partner organizations have launched an awareness-raising campaign about the consequences of marriage at an early age. It is being led by the Women's National Committee (WNC), the Women's Studies and Development Centre, and a network of local organizations called the 'Shima Network'.

Because justifications for marriage at an early age are rooted in cultural and religious traditions, it is not going to be an easy issue to challenge. But these groups are prepared to speak out. Public education through such means as plays, leaflets, and media coverage, will be combined with campaigning work, calling on the government to adopt 18 as the minimum legal age for marriage.

'We have buried our heads in the sand for too long', says the WNC's Hooria Mashoor. 'Early marriage jeopardizes development. We can't ignore it. We have to have courage to face this issue.'

Other key points that the 2004 workshop established are that:

- Individuals have multiple, intersecting identities, including gender, class, age, culture, and ethnicity. Some are owned, and others perceived. Labelling which only focuses on one aspect of identity can have a negative impact on women's rights as it hides the diversity of needs and roles that women have based on their multiple identities;
- Religious 'fundamentalism', discrimination, stereotyping and political instability are some of the many factors obstructing work to promote gender equality;
- There is a need to respond using local knowledge to adapt the broad and shared human rights framework to tackle specific local development needs;
- When talking about 'Muslim contexts', we should bear in mind that contexts are constantly evolving, and that our understanding of context is both time- and place-specific, and subjective.

Changes in contexts

Two years later, in February 2006, Oxfam GB again brought together a group of staff from a cross-section of countries, including Bangladesh, India, Pakistan, Palestinian Territories, Philippines, Sudan, Tajikistan, Tanzania, and the UK. This workshop aimed to deepen the analysis of the previous workshop and to share learning on practical development interventions and responses at programme level.

The second workshop began by identifying the changes that have occurred – globally, nationally and locally – over the two years since the previous workshop. Some of the points identified by participants were:

- Some extremist fundamentalist groups are using the global political situation to justify and increase their strength; often the war in Iraq and atrocities against Muslims in other places are used to justify their point;
- Military action involving Western forces in several Muslim countries has exacerbated a perception amongst some people that all organizations

originating in the West, including international NGOs, are hostile to Islam. This can present security challenges for Oxfam staff;

- There is an increasing withdrawal of civil liberties and erosion of women's rights and a concurrent rise in 'fundamentalist' interpretations of Islam and other religions across the globe;
- Some Muslim fundamentalist groups are using their involvement in disaster relief to introduce narrower interpretations and definitions of Islam – often these target women's dress, mobility, and behaviour;
- The global debate on identity politics has come to the fore in the UK since the bombings of July 2005 in London;
- While discrimination against Muslim groups continues, there is a greater effort to understand 'fundamentalism' and Muslim contexts, while also becoming aware of the complexities of engaging with 'religious groups'.

Challenges for work on gender equality in Muslim contexts

Specific challenges to gender equality identified by participants included early or child marriage; a lack of choice in marriage; imposition of dress codes; male migration resulting in desertion, polygamy, and additional burdens on women-headed households; and restrictions on girls' education and women's mobility justified with reference to religion. Many of these challenges are common to different contexts and locations. Other challenges identified, although not experienced by all participants in their countries, include:

- Ensuring development initiatives reach marginalized communities, and difficulties in persuading governments to allocate sufficient resources to promoting gender equality in development;
- Contradictions between the ideal and reality of women's roles in society, and how to change women's own attitudes;
- A lack of social and political alternatives to the fundamentalist vision;
- Rising 'fundamentalisms' and communities of men and women seeing themselves in terms of narrowly defined religious identities, rather than taking rights-based positions on their development needs.

There is an undeniable global focus on Islam, and increasingly narrow definitions of Islam promoted by the international media, countries and 'fundamentalists'. This has brought a greater urgency to specifically understanding challenges facing gender work in Muslim contexts, even if there remains a need to question the intentions behind this focus. These challenges include the fact that understandings of what is and what is not acceptable 'behaviour' by women are dominated by conservative, male opinion. This is because in most Muslim contexts, women are not permitted to engage in religious interpretation and are generally silenced, whereas men who engage in progressive interpretation may face condemnation and violence. This makes the challenge of protecting the space for dissent and alternative voices, including progressive interpretations of Islam, extremely important, given the tendency of the media to overlook such progressive interpretations, as these do not produce the kind of headlines that match stereotyped visions of Islam. This does not help the popularization of progressive, gender-friendly interpretations globally, and assists in keeping them invisible locally. Finally, in some places where Muslims are a minority community, there are additional or particular challenges, as there may be parallel legal systems for different communities.

Successful strategies for promoting gender equality

Despite these challenges, Oxfam GB staff have worked to achieve progress in promoting gender equality in various programmes in Muslim contexts around the globe, and the workshops were able to draw out some of the strategies employed by different teams. Indeed, discussions highlighted that despite the common perception of religion as a barrier to gender equality, it can also present opportunities.

Showing the links between gender equality and Islam

Some of Oxfam's programme teams have found that using religious arguments to promote gender equality is an effective strategy. Many local NGOs working in Muslim countries, both secular and faith-based, have similarly found that using a religious framework has been an effective strategy to bring about social change. The following example from Oxfam's Pakistan programme illustrates this well (Box 5.2).

Box 5.2 Improving girls' education in Makhi, Pakistan

The remote desert area of Makhi and Achhro Thar in Sanghar District is 300 km north-east of Karachi. With no irrigation facilities, few roads, and no public transport, the area, which has a population of around 70,000, is one of the poorest regions of Sindh Province. The community is reliant on subsistence agriculture, cattle herding, and fishing, and has been sorely neglected by the government and political parties. The literacy rates in Achhro Thar are extremely low. Overall, only 5 per cent of people are literate – and only 0.3 per cent of women.

With Oxfam's support, the Makhi Welfare Organization opened schools in seven villages and started classes in September 2000. Within six months, 34 boys and 49 girls out of the 191 children enrolled at that time passed their first exam and were promoted to the next class. The total enrolment is now 274, of whom 168 are girls. For the first time there are girls and boys in the villages who can read and write.

Prior to the project, villagers had been opposed to girls' education, considering it a waste of time and money, and showed little interest in educating boys either. They did not think that education was relevant to their lives. However, MWO's social mobilization and awareness-raising activities convinced village elders of the importance of sending girls to school. The children, too, are enthusiastic about their education. Girls told project workers how they work during the cotton-picking season to earn money to buy their uniforms and schoolbooks. One girl explained: 'I want to study further and want to be a doctor, if the financial situation of my family would allow this to happen.'

The most successful strategy adopted by MWO has been to use arguments from Islamic texts, which state that men and women should be educated. They have also played cassettes of speeches by the community's spiritual leader, in which he asks followers to send both boys and girls to school. The MWO team are all from the area, which has made it easier for them to gain the villagers' confidence.

The community has developed a strong sense of ownership towards the schools and many are now also participating in meetings and seminars about education. They are involved in the running of the schools and have constructed buildings and provided furniture. Through the project, villagers have become aware of their own socio-economic rights and have a growing determination to improve their lives. People from villages outside the project area have also been encouraged to start sending girls to school.

Taking a secular approach

There is undoubtedly a need to recognize religion as an issue in Oxfam's work. However, not all strategies need to refer to religion – sometimes secular frameworks can be just as effective, as illustrated by the example of Oxfam's work in Bangladesh (Box 5.3, overleaf).

The important lesson to take from these two case studies is to base programme strategies on an analysis of what approach is appropriate and likely to be effective in a given context at a given time.

Interestingly, the Bangladesh context is rapidly changing and faith-based groups are gaining power throughout the country. Oxfam took a deliberate decision to adopt a secular, non-threatening approach when initiating the campaign to encourage families to eat a meal together, but the programme team is finding it increasingly necessary to frame their work in religious terms – to 'prove' that their work on gender equality is compatible with Islam – in order to gain acceptance in the communities in which they work.

Box 5.3 Campaigning for families to eat a meal together

Oxfam's gender equality programme in Bangladesh, working with partner organization Polli Sree, has taken an indirect approach to addressing women's rights. Rather than tackling unequal power relations through a religious framework, the programme launched a campaign focusing on the simple message of the family, women and men, eating meals together at least once a day.

The idea was born out of concerns that the traditional practice of women eating whatever food is left over, after everyone else has eaten, was having a negative impact on the health of women generally, and on pregnant women and their babies in particular. Polli Sree initiated discussions with group members, who at first were sceptical, and thought it right that men should eat first, as they are the main wage earners in the family. But following further discussions, more and more participants gradually began to accept that eating together would bring benefits for the whole family.

The campaign initially met with resistance from both men and women, but ongoing dialogue and communications work has successfully challenged entrenched social beliefs and practices. It has improved nutrition for women and girls, and encouraged a sense of equality in the household by creating time for conversation, thus allowing women more access to decision-making in the household. It has also helped to challenge patriarchal hierarchy within the family, and increase women's confidence in thinking about equality.

Identifying key allies

The Pakistan case study clearly shows the positive gains that can be made by gaining the support of religious and community leaders. Oxfam GB's Indonesia programme has also found that bringing on board key allies is an important strategy, although they have taken an indirect route to reaching local decision-makers (Box 5.4).

At the workshops participants explored in some depth whether it was desirable for Oxfam GB's programmes to engage with faith-based groups, and what such engagement might involve. It was concluded that Oxfam's secular position does not imply that the organization does not work with faith-based groups, and indeed Oxfam GB already does so, for example, partnering with Christian organizations on community development projects in various parts of the world.[2] The essential criteria in forming such partnerships should not be the religious identity of the organization but its goals and position on human rights, tolerance of religious diversity and poverty alleviation; in other words, its compatibility with Oxfam's own mission and values, including Oxfam's organizational commitment to diversity and gender equality.

Box 5.4 Working with key allies in Madura, Indonesia

The Indonesia education programme operates in a strict Muslim area that places low priority on girls' education. The strategy started with the identification of the main actors that would lead and support the initiative. The programme team chose to work with the women's chapter of the largest Muslim organization in the country, with the intention to first influence women themselves, and to increase their awareness of the importance of using their own education to educate others. Most of these women leaders are university graduates, but as they too are influenced by social stereotypes about the value of girls' education, they don't use their position to promote education in their area. Another consideration was the fact that many of these women are married to religious leaders or to men who hold key positions in local government, and so it was hoped that the women would indirectly influence the male-dominated local policy environment.

Listening to women's voices

If Oxfam's work is to successfully promote gender equality in Muslim contexts we must, first and foremost, listen to Muslim women speak about their own needs and concerns, and take time to find out their perspective on the issues they face. Oxfam's UK Poverty Programme (UKPP) is doing just this, as they begin to design a programme to tackle gender and race inequalities faced by Muslim women in the north of England (see Box 5.5).

Box 5.5 Removing barriers to south Asian women's employment

In the UK, Muslims make up 3 per cent of the population (1.6 million) and almost 40 per cent of the ethnic minority population. Muslim women belong to the most disadvantaged faith community in the UK. Their unemployment rate is three times the national average, and they have a higher economic inactivity rate than women of any other faith group. As an ethnic group, Muslims are more likely to live in poor areas, be unemployed, have low incomes, achieve low educational attainment, live in poor housing, report ill-health and be victims of crime. Since the London bombings in July 2005, carried out by young British-born Muslim men, the further rise in Islamophobia has led to Muslim women feeling increasingly isolated in many ways, and being forced to defend their faith. According to Ahmed et al. (2005: 7) 'this inevitably affects the human, social and economic capital of individuals residing in the community which will impact on Muslim women's choices and commitments'.

Social Enterprise Development Initiative (SEDI), one of Oxfam's partners working with Muslim communities, carried out research to identify the experiences of Muslim women in accessing the labour market in the north-west region of England in 2005.

There are increasing numbers of Muslim women living in Britain reasserting a self-conscious Islamic identity. By adopting the *hijab* as a symbol of resistance towards male attention, many Muslim women feel able to move freely in the public sphere. There is a pervasive view that Muslim women are silenced, oppressed and controlled by men, and references to the barriers to employment Muslim women face are often made in this context. However, Muslim women are diverse, and the barriers that they face vary greatly. And these barriers are not necessarily related to men. Nevertheless, many of the women who participated in this research also felt that how and where they spent their time depended on socially constructed attitudes and stereotypes of gender roles, that either enabled or restricted their choices. SEDI's main research findings were as follows:

- Widespread views and comments that those who are 'visibly' Muslim in terms of dress and behaviour are more likely to be affected by religious discrimination. This can affect their experiences in the labour market.
- Many Muslim women have no direct objection to entering the labour market, or undertaking education and training, but see flexibility, particularly for women with children, as the key requirement to their working outside the home.
- Those Muslim women who have engaged in further education or gained further qualification are the most determined to work and manage childcare at the same time.
- Family, friends, and the community can at times have a significant effect on the field of work and study Muslim women can enter.
- Many Muslim women are confident about setting up their own businesses, but lack assistance and understanding from UK service providers, including business advice specialists, and often lack encouragement and support from family members.
- The cumulative barriers to employment impact unfavourably on Muslim women's self-esteem and confidence, and 'lack of experience' is the most cited reason given for the difficulties Muslim women encounter in securing employment.

What next for Oxfam?

The workshop participants identified a number of key challenges that Oxfam will need to face up to as we develop this area of work further.

Oxfam's image

The 'war on terror' has affected the work of Oxfam employees in many countries, and created difficulties for them. Some of the workshop participants gave examples of how the UK government's military involvement in Iraq and Afghanistan has made it necessary for Oxfam to keep a lower profile as a British NGO in their countries, and to undertake advocacy work to clarify Oxfam's independence from the UK government. Oxfam staff members have needed to explain their activities very clearly, be transparent about sources of funding, and counteract local views of British people and organizations being anti-Islam.

> As an international NGO, we have to be particularly careful to ensure that when we work on sensitive issues like violence against women, the actual implementation of our initiatives is undertaken by appropriate local organizations. If we fail to do this, we run the risk of being accused of interference and introducing 'foreign' ideas that are not appropriate to the local cultural and religious context. (M. B. Akhter, Gender Programme Co-ordinator, Bangladesh)

Framing programmes in terms of human rights

Oxfam is committed to a rights-based approach to development, but it is not always possible for staff to use human rights language in their work. Participants at the workshops felt that the UN had lost credibility in many of the communities in which they work, and that as a result human rights treaties are increasingly being dismissed as a 'Western imposition'.

This is true of women's rights, which have been labelled as a Western idea, irrelevant to local culture, and so have met with resistance from both men and women. The challenge lies in how to present women's rights programmes in a way that is accepted by local communities. Using quotes from the Koran (as in the Pakistan case study) or examples from other countries, that demonstrate that women's rights are compatible with Islam, may be a pragmatic strategy, although this is very much dependent on the local context.

Extending our analysis to other religions

Participants were clear on the need to extend discussions of gender and identity politics beyond Muslim contexts. All religious contexts exert pressure on the development agenda, and our work would benefit from inviting more perspectives on this debate. We are taking this into account in our strategic planning on our gender equality work for 2007–10.

Conclusion: understanding the interaction between religion and tradition, gender inequality, and development

In many of Oxfam's programmes, staff have an inadequate understanding and appreciation of the diversity of Muslim contexts, and of the links between gender inequality, faith, and development. In some instances, expatriate staff may use their lack of understanding as an excuse to do nothing – 'not wanting to interfere in local culture'. However, Oxfam has a clearly stated commitment to addressing gender inequality in all our work, and so this gap in understanding needs to be addressed.

Box 5.6 Raising awareness of gender issues among Oxfam staff in Afghanistan

In 2002, the return of relative stability to Afghanistan gave Oxfam staff the space to focus on issues beyond emergency work. It was at this point that a two-member gender team was put in place. Their role was to address the major gap in the team's understanding of concepts such as gender roles and gender equality. Without this knowledge, members of staff were finding it difficult to challenge existing gender roles and promote women's rights in the communities with whom they worked.

As a result, Oxfam staff have participated in more than 20 workshops and training sessions, to consider the links between gender inequality and poverty, and to understand concepts like gender indicators and gender-disaggregated monitoring and evaluation. All relevant documents, including Oxfam's gender policy and tool kits, have been translated into the local languages for staff to use, and have been incorporated into inductions for new staff.

The overall conclusion of Oxfam's workshops has been that there is a need to emphasize and understand the local context, and how specific issues affect gender relations on the ground in each country, and consider the way in which the global context intersects with local politics and existing practices that obstruct or promote gender equality.

Notes

1   To protect the woman's identity, her name has been changed.
2   Oxfam works closely with a wide range of faith-based organizations, including Islamic Relief in its development education work. In addition, as a member of the Make Poverty History/Global Call to Action Against Poverty, Oxfam GB partnered Muslim, Hindu, Buddhist and Jewish groups.

Reference

Ahmed, J., Allaand, A. and Hussain, Z. (2005) *Faith and Enterprise: a study to investigate the barriers to employment for Muslim women in the North West,* SEDI, Manchester.

Acknowledgements

The authors would like to acknowledge the following people, for their help in the putting together of this chapter: Mona Mehta, Cassandra Balchin, Freshta Sayed, Mohammed Badi Akhter, Yanti Lacsana, Elaine Bible, Shazia Nizamani and Ehsan Leghari.

About the authors

Adrienne Hopkins works in Oxfam GB's Programme Resource Centre, supporting programme staff to access relevant tools and resources, and share information and experience on gender equality programming.

Kirit Patel is the Race Equality Programme Co-ordinator for the Oxfam UK Poverty Programme. He is working to develop and strengthen partnerships with black and minority ethnic NGOs and networks in tackling the inequalities and poverty experienced by their communities in the UK.

Chapter 6

Christianity, development, and women's liberation

Bridget Walker

This chapter first appeared in *Gender & Development* Volume 7, Issue 1, March 1999, p. 15–22

Development practitioners working for gender equity must understand the significance of religion for many women who live in poverty. Both development interventions and religion are concerned with poverty; and both have often been problematic for women. Religious faith can offer women the opportunity for liberation; but it can also encourage conformity.

Introduction

'I was active in the church throughout the 20 years of my marriage, during which I lived in constant fear ... The church was my lifeline ... It was the only place my husband allowed me to go ... but these (the church's) messages helped me stay in that relationship of fear for a long time' (quoted in Gnanadason 1997: 45).

This quotation illustrates the ambiguous nature of the support offered to women by religious institutions. For this woman, trapped in a violent relationship, the Christian church provided the only chance to associate with others and to escape temporarily from the prison of her home – yet it did not offer her liberation. On the other hand, religion has been a resource in struggles for equality and emancipation for many women. Gender and development workers must be aware of these two options – domestication and liberation – because on the one hand, religious teaching preaches women's subordination through imposing social codes regarding women's roles, behaviour, and relationships with men. On the other hand, church may also offer the only space in which women can meet.

While religion may seem remote and even irrelevant to increasing numbers of people in Britain (my own context) it is an important force in the lives of many people on other continents. It is of personal significance, providing rituals at deeply emotional moments of birth, marriage, and death. It offers opportunities for reflecting on the meaning and purpose of life, and an explanation for suffering. It prescribes codes of behaviour in the family and beyond, and provides a means of expressing a communal identity. It may shape the nature of the state, and influence the way the economy is run. On the other hand, religion offers alternatives to the dominant models of social, economic, and political development (White and Tiongco 1997). Many Christians in Latin America have turned to the messages which liberation theology has for those living in poverty or under oppression; others, in both Americas, have embraced Christian fundamentalism.

I focus on the Christian tradition, because it is the one I know best: it has shaped the society in which I live, the communities among whom I have worked, and my own thinking as a feminist and a development worker. I shall look primarily, but not exclusively, at the tradition and legacy of the churches which emerged in the West[1] and missionized the Americas, Africa, and Asia. I shall examine briefly what these churches have to say about the nature of women, family relations, and other social institutions, and how women in the South have responded.

Christianity and 'development'

Christians have always described development in terms which go beyond conventional definitions of development as modernization and economic growth. The papal encyclical Populorum Progressio (1967) claimed development as a new name for peace. A Christian Aid pamphlet[2] published in 1970 states: 'Development means growth towards wholeness: it describes the process by which individual persons and communities struggle to realize their full potential; physical and intellectual, cultural and spiritual, social and political. Thus, development is a Christian concern' (Christian Aid 1970: 5).

However, in countries of the South, development interventions have succeeded colonialism, which was influenced by the Christian missionary activities of imperial powers. Religious authority has often been allied with social, political, and economic power. As a consequence, theological doctrine has reflected establishment interests, given ideological support for the rise of capitalism, and, through missionary activity, imposed a Western worldview on the religious consciousness of other cultures. 'When white people came to South Africa, they had the Bible, and we had the land. But now we find that they have the land and we have the Bible' (Roxanne Jordaan in King 1994: 155).

However, there have always been challenges to the religious institutions of the establishment. In Europe in the sixteenth century, movements to reform the doctrines and institutions of the Christian church claimed the word of God in the scriptures as the supreme authority, thus challenging the priestly hierarchy. The Bible became accessible to people in their own languages and their own homes. It continues to be a resource for Christians working for change today. The Jubilee 2000 Coalition[3] is an international movement of churches and development agencies which bases its messages about the cancellation of Third World debt on the biblical imperative of justice for the poor. In Africa, Christians have sought an authentic, 'decolonized' theology, while in Asia the struggle for human rights has focused the thinking of

Christian men and women. The church in the Philippines was divided during the years of repression: the establishment supported the state, while many individual Protestants and Catholics joined Muslims and Marxists in the people's struggle for change (Duremdes 1989: 38). Throughout Latin America, a theology has emerged which explicitly names itself a theology of libera-tion.[4] In situations where there was no freedom to speak directly about the political and economic situation in Latin America, it was still possible to tell stories from the Bible. People immediately understood the messages of the Old Testament prophets who condemned unjust landlords, the sharp practice of profiteers, and the corruption of the courts; they identified with the gospel narratives of the New Testament in which the sick are healed, the hungry fed, outcasts are befriended, and which presents a vision of a kingdom of justice and love. Liberation theology has influenced current development thinking about participation and empowerment (Eade 1997). I return to consider women's relationship to liberation theology in the next section

Christianity, women, and social institutions

In this section, I examine the opportunities and constraints which exist for women in the tradition of mainstream Christianity regarding their sexuality and family life – at community level, within the church itself and in convent life, in the economy, and at the wider national and international levels.

Sexuality and the family

The churches have often interpreted human nature in a manner that is profoundly damaging to women. In particular, the control of female sexuality is of concern to patriarchal society: this control is expressed in many religious and cultural forms. Christianity may be used to deprive women of autonomy over their own bodies, for example, through the prohibition of abortion (as in the case where the Pope, head of the Roman Catholic church, advised the Archbishop of Sarajevo that the women who had been raped had a duty to bear the children thus conceived (Gnanadason 1997). The negative impact of this attitude not only affects women at the level of their personal and social relations, but also shapes the legislation of states which have a Christian tradi-tion which makes women subordinated, second-class citizens.

The fact that women often seek support from the churches in family matters is ironic, considering their record. Aruna Gnanadason, of the World Council of Churches, has commented: 'Our concerns have been the sanctity of the family, reconciliation, restoring marriages, when often the first need is for an end to violence, for safety for women and children, and for justice for the oppressed' (Gnanadason 1997: 43).

From 1988 to 1998, Christian churches took part in the Ecumenical Decade of Churches in Solidarity with Women, which was designed to keep alive the concerns of the UN Women's Decade (1975–85). One of its activities was a four-year process of visiting all members of the World Council of Churches (WCC) and analysing the findings from these visits. The teams (usually two women, two men, and a WCC staff member) met church leaders, members of congregations, students and teachers of theology. The WCC's main topics of research mirrored the priorities of the UN Women's Decade: violence against women; women's full participation in the life of the church; the global economic crisis and its effects on women; racism and xenophobia and their effects on women.

More than 200 people were engaged in making the visits. Each team wrote its own report, which was then forwarded to the church concerned. *Living Letters*, published by the WCC in 1997, is a digest of these reports with extensive quotations from the discussions.[5] In *Living Letters*, the authors comment that the dominant model of the family they encountered was a traditional, hierarchical, and patriarchal one, in which women played a submissive role.

A different view of women's role in family and society can sometimes be conveyed effectively through discussions of gender issues in development. At a gender-training workshop in which I participated, organized by Oxfam GB in Kenya some years ago, we discussed women's and men's roles in the home and in agriculture, and their different workloads. The values underlying Oxfam's work in development were discussed, such as the need for everyone's participation – men's and women's – in planning processes and in making decision which would affect their lives. There was a lively discussion of these issues, with much use by participants of scriptural references to support their points of view. A proverb which suggested that beating and love were connected was firmly repudiated by a participant who quoted the Bible. Love, she said, is patient and kind.[6] In the closing session, a church leader who had at the outset quoted scriptural references to support male authority, and who had claimed that the equality of women and men was 'against God and nature', said thoughtfully that he needed to rethink the way in which his church was governed, and his role in it. Perhaps, he said, he should not be doing everything himself.

Mercy Oduyoye, a theologian from Ghana, comments caustically: 'African men sing "Viva" when people talk about racial and class exploitation, but they can hang you if you dare talk about sexism. They say African culture legitimates it and, if they are Christians, sections of the Bible seal it for them' (King 1994: 66). Women become dangerous when they question patriarchal models in this way, for this is to question the foundation of institutions as broad as the state and as intimate as the family. Christian feminists may be regarded by men and women alike as destructive of relationships, the family and all that is sacred.

Organization and leadership in the churches

Throughout most of history, the Christian churches have been run by men, and leadership is still largely in men's hands. Yet, paradoxically, many churches have also provided the opportunity for women to meet, discuss, organize, and learn new skills. Rigoberta Menchu, the Guatemalan revolutionary leader, describes in her autobiography how, at the age of 12, she became a lay preacher, and how the church provided her with the opportunity to develop leadership qualities and to organize (Burgos Debray 1984). However, she criticizes the way in which the priests encouraged her people to remain passive and accept the status quo. Menchu calls for a church of the people, organized by them, and reflecting their experience of hunger and oppression. She sees this church as more than a building or an organizational structure; it is a real change within people. This change should also address the relations between women and men and the 'machismo' (male attitude of domination) which she likens to a sickness. Ofelia Ortega from Cuba[7] argues that the contribution of Latin American women is essential for the maturity of liberation theology. Its message of good news and deliverance from bondage for the poor must reflect poor women's experience and needs. In the Christian Base Communities[8] of Latin America, women are represented in significant numbers – the structure of organization is more participatory, and less formal, clerical, and hierarchical than in the traditional church. Here women are free to read and reflect on the Bible from their own perspective and to relate it to their own lives.

Religious orders: an alternative model of community

The convent may at first glance seem an unlikely launch pad for women's liberation. Yet some women in Europe struggling for the right to vote in the nineteenth century looked back on the convents of the past and claimed that 400 years earlier, these had been communities in which women could develop their potential and serve society. Religious women today suggest that religious communities represent an alternative 'corporate' model in social structures which remain dominated by men, and which still position women in family or kinship groups, and identify them as daughters, wives, and mothers.

The church in the marketplace

While the members of religious orders usually make vows of poverty, Christian religious foundations often hold substantial company shares to provide income. In Britain, Canada and the United States, religious women have played a key role in shareholder action[9], challenging transnational corporations (TNCs) to take ethical considerations into account in their operations in countries of the South. This challenge is one form of working in solidarity with those women and men struggling for the liberation of Third World countries. Sharon Ruiz Duremdes from the Philippines, writing in *Women in a Changing World* (WCC Women's Unit 1989), sees this as an important way of 'doing theology' for women in the countries of the North.

International networking for change in the churches

The WCC has supported a range of global initiatives focusing on women, of which the Ecumenical Decade of Churches in Solidarity with Women has been one of the most far-reaching, challenging member churches and providing a voice for women of faith. Theirs is a voice of critical solidarity. *Living Letters* (WCC 1997) makes a series of recommendations to churches. One of them argues that the churches should denounce violence against women, regardless of whether it is culturally sanctioned; another that they should recognize the links between sexism and racism, and combat them at the centre of church life. Another recommendation is that economic injustice against women should be addressed through development programmes and advocacy concerning the root causes of women's poverty. Economic justice must also be practised in the way churches are run, through equal opportunities and equal pay. The forms and substance of religious practice need to be re-examined in the light of women's experience and perspective, and their need for liberation.

The voices of women

What are women themselves saying about religion today? In many social contexts, 'feminism' remains a suspect and threatening concept, and many women would reject the title of feminist, while nevertheless following the first principle of feminist theology – being faithful to their own experience. There are a number of positions which I would like to categorize, rather crudely, as follows: re-affirming the faith; reclaiming it; reforming it; and rejecting it.

Re-affirming the faith

Women in the Orthodox churches have argued that it is possible to be faithful to church tradition, and work for change within it. The Living Letters initiative found that, in Russia, the specificity of the roles of women and men means that, in the parishes, the priest has a mostly spiritual role, whereas the administrative decisions are taken by women, who run the parish council. Women are active in social work and in religious education; they feel that their contribution is recognized and appreciated (WCC 1997).

At times of personal or political upheaval, women may choose to reaffirm their religious affiliation. This may be a source of solace, or offer a form of identity; it may be a conservative or a radical move, or it may, paradoxically, contain elements of both. For example, women and men who supported the Catholic church in Poland in the days of the Cold War were participating in religious practice which presented a radical challenge to the Marxist government of the day, yet the Polish church remained deeply conservative in its attitude to women. 'Resistance theology', like 'resistance politics', has seldom reflected women's interests until challenged to do so by women in the movements.

Reclaiming the faith

It has been important for many women of different traditions of faith, including Christianity, to return to the roots of religious belief, in order to analyse how some aspects have been given prominence by religious institutions, while others have been ignored. They argue that men have used religion to serve their patriarchal purposes, but that there is a more woman-friendly tradition to be reclaimed: the early Christians lived in an egalitarian community of women and men,[10] and women held positions of leadership. Christian women have looked for liberating models in the Bible: Deborah the Judge and Esther the Queen in the Old Testament, and the women in the community around Jesus in the New Testament. Mary, so often presented as an impossible ideal of the woman as virgin and mother, is reclaimed as the strong 'female face' of the faith, proclaiming the reversal of the established order: 'he [i.e., God] has pulled down princes from their thrones and exalted the lowly; the hungry he has filled with good things, and the rich sent empty away' (Luke 1: 52–3). The Bible offers a diversity of images of God, from which the church has selected mainly masculine terms; feminist theologians argue that to name God only in terms of father, warrior, king, and lord is to limit our understanding of the divine–human relationship. Ofelia Ortega suggests that this task of reclaiming also is important for men, whose spirituality she sees as having been damaged by the distortion of biblical revelation (WCC 1989).

Reforming the faith

Many feminist theologians argue that reclaiming the faith is not enough, because religions arise in specific historical contexts, and are formed by the political and economic forces and social attitudes of the time. Therefore, the codes and practices developed at one time need to be reformed for a changed social context. Movements for the ordination of women have used this argument. Feminist theology takes as its starting point the search for women's identity, grounded in women's own experience, rather than in the forms imposed by a patriarchal culture. This leads to personal and social transformation.

Women theologians of the South have also stressed the necessity of addressing the inheritance of cultural and spiritual imperialism from the missionary endeavours which brought Christianity to continents including Africa. Teresa Hinga, from Kenya, sees Christ as an ambivalent figure for African women: he is both conqueror and liberator. She suggests that it was the latter perception of Christ and the 'emancipatory impulses' within missionary Christianity which led to a positive response from Africans. Hinga quotes the example of women among the Kamba of Kenya, who tried to break away from unsatisfactory marriages or harsh parental control by seeking refuge with the Africa Inland Mission, a Protestant mission in that area (Hinga 1994).

Another important focus for feminist theologians has been that of language: the translation of the Bible, and the words of the liturgy. Gnanadason argues that the images of God in Western Christianity are based on the 'social norms and gender role specifics in that culture's national, ecclesiastical, business and family level' (Gnanadason 1989: 29). Drawing on examples from India, she points out the need to move beyond the conventional masculine image of God, asserting that God can be depicted in alternative, and female forms; and that new and diverse models of God should be developed to include the experience of all peoples.

Rejecting the faith of the fathers

Many women reject organized religion because they see it as part and parcel of a profoundly contaminating patriarchy, built on, and maintained by, violence. The Christian churches are judged to have been complicit in the violence of colonialism in the past and genocide in this century. But women from formerly-colonised countries, whose consciousness has been formed in a Christian tradition, continue to seek means of articulation of their spiritual experience, often drawing on their Christian heritage. Oduyoye looks at the tradition of independent Christian movements which have emerged in opposition to the racism and ethnocentrism of Euro-Americans on the African continent. At some churches, African Christian women have tapped into the primal religious sources of their communities, for example through the healing ministry of a prophetess.

Conclusion

At the beginning of this chapter, I stated that those concerned with social development and social justice should analyse the role of religious institutions in the lives of women, and understand their relationship to them. I have outlined how the traditions of the Christian church have often demeaned women, but have also, paradoxically, supported them within the parameters of existing social structures. Through a brief discussion of how women have claimed liberation from a perspective grounded in their faith, I have examined different perspectives on the extent to which forms of Christianity offer scope for women's liberation or oppression. Women's continued critique of Christianity demonstrates that their relationship with it is more often one of engagement than rejection. Development workers concerned with the struggle against poverty and its causes, and with improving the quality of life for all, must listen to what women are saying about the spiritual as well as the material dimension of their lives.

Notes

1   The Christian church was established as the religion of the Roman Empire by the end of the fourth century. It split into two major groups: the Eastern (Orthodox) church, and the Western church with the Bishop

of Rome (the Roman Catholic Pope) at its head. The Roman Catholic church was subsequently split by reform movements which led to the establishment of Protestant churches. (There are also smaller churches with an ancient history, such as the Nestorians, the Copts (Egypt), and the Ethiopian church. All these, like the Eastern Orthodox church, generally did not expand through missionary activity in the same way as the Western churches.)

2 Jay, Eric (1970) *World Development and the Bible*, Christian Aid: London.

3 Jubilee 2000 is an international movement of development agencies and church bodies calling for the cancellation of the unpayable debts of the poorest countries by the year 2000. For a description of the Year of Jubilee, when debts are written off, see Leviticus 25: 8–17.

4 At a meeting in Medellin in 1968, the Roman Catholic Bishops of Latin America denounced the unjust maintenance of wealth by a few at the expense of the majority of citizens, and placed themselves firmly on the side of the poor, according to the Gospel's imperative to bring good news to the poor, proclaim liberty to the captives, and to set free the downtrodden (Luke 4: 18–19). Liberation theology started from the position of the oppressed and the poor seeking liberation. The expression 'liberation theology' was used by the Peruvian theologian Gustavo Gutierrez.

5 The booklet was also the result of a team effort and no single author. The foreword is written by Nicole Fischer-Duchable, the WCC consultant to the Mid Decade Process.

6 1 Corinthians 13: 10–12.

7 'Women doing Theology and Sharing Spirituality', pp. 10–11 in *Women in a Changing World*, Issue 28, WCC: Geneva.

8 The Christian Base Communities are a feature of liberation theology in practice. Grassroots groups within the Catholic Church meet to reflect on the Bible and the teachings of Jesus as these relate to their own lives. They have provided an opportunity for women to organize, to participate in decision making, and to enjoy a freedom they may not have at home.

9 Shareholder action bodies such as the Interfaith Committee on Corporate Responsibility in the USA, and the Ecumenical Council for Corporate Responsibility in the UK, encourage churches and religious foundations with investments to raise ethical questions at annual general shareholder meetings, and to engage in dialogue about the companies' operations in the South.

10 Acts 4: 32–5; see also Gnanadason (WCC 1989: 30).

References

Burgos Debray, E. (ed) (1984) *I, Rigoberta Menchu*, Verso: London.

Duremdes, S.R. (1989) 'Women in Theology: Philippine Perspectives' in *Women in a Changing World*, 28, WCC: Geneva.

Eade, D. (1998) *Capacity Building: An Approach to People Centred Development*, Oxfam GB: Oxford.

Gnanadason, A. (1997) *No Longer a Secret: The Church and Violence against Women*, WCC: Geneva.

Gutierrez, G. (1983) *The Power of the Poor in History,* SCM: London.

Hinga, T. (1994) 'Jesus Christ and the Liberation of Women in Africa' in King, U. (ed.) *Feminist Theology from the Third World,* SPCK: London.

IDOC and the Commission of the Churches on International Affairs, *Human Rights: A Challenge to Theology,* Rome.

Jordaan, R. (1994) 'Black Feminist Theology in South Africa' in King, U. (ed.) *Feminist Theology from the Third World,* SPCK: London.

Ortega, Ofelia (1995) *Women's Visions: Theological Reflection, Celebration, Action,* WCC: Geneva.

Taylor, Michael (1990) *Good for the Poor: Christian Ethics and World Development,* Mowbray: London.

The Jerusalem Bible (1986) Darton, Longman and Todd: London.

WCC Women's Unit (1989) 'Women doing Theology and Sharing Spirituality' in *Women in a Changing World,* 28, WCC: Geneva.

White, S. and Tiongco, R. (1997) *Doing Theology and Development,* Saint Andrew Press: Edinburgh.

About the author

Bridget Walker is a Responding to Conflict Associate and is a trustee of Christian Aid. She has been a member of the Strategic Planning and Evaluation team at Oxfam GB and was previously an adviser in Oxfam's Gender and Development Unit.

Chapter 7

Conflict and compliance: Christianity and the occult in horticultural exporting

Catherine S. Dolan

This chapter first appeared in *Gender & Development* Volume 7, Issue 1, March 1999, p. 23–30

The introduction of new export crops in the early 1990s upset the customary division of labour between men and women in Meru District, Kenya, and led to conflict over land, labour, and income. Women's workload increased; their earnings did not. They responded by turning to 'born-again' Christianity for support, and by resorting to traditional witchcraft to regain control.

Religion and witchcraft are often perceived as peripheral to developmental objectives. At best, they are considered interesting phenomena of social life; at worst, they are viewed as relics of societies out of step with the modern world. Development practitioners tend to view religion as a static feature of culture, with little relevance to the success of development interventions (Mukhopadhyay 1995). Drawing on research conducted from 1994–96 and briefly in 1998, this chapter challenges this assumption: in Meru District, Kenya, the introduction of export horticulture has generated conflict over land, labour, and income, and women use witchcraft and Christianity to mitigate intra-household struggles over income from export crops. Women are responding to the erosion of their rights in ways that may appear paradoxical: some undergo Christian conversion, while others bewitch and poison their husbands. Some do both. These practices simultaneously comply with male authority, and resist it.

While the region has a long history of export-oriented agriculture (coffee and tea), it had become one of the largest French bean-producing areas in Kenya by the 1990s. This has had a profound effect on female farmers. Prior to the introduction of French beans, women's land (conventionally very small plots) was used to grow vegetables for household consumption and for sale at local markets. In response to pressure for agricultural diversification to supply the expanding European market for 'gourmet' vegetables, horticulture – historically a female domain – has been rapidly intensified, commoditized, and, in many cases, appropriated by men. The profitability of French beans grown for the export market is raising the stakes in horticultural production; men usurp either the land allocated for, or the income derived from, French bean production. The customary division of labour by crop and gender is currently undergoing a sea-change, as tensions escalate over male and female property rights and women's contributions to household subsistence.

The spiritual domain has become a principal forum through which struggles over land and labour are expressed; these struggles can undermine the developmental objectives of export horticulture.

Global food networks and gender relations

Until the 1980s, food consumption patterns of urban populations in the West were limited by the seasonal availability of locally grown fresh produce. In contrast, today agro-food chains deliver fresh fruits and vegetables from all over the world to Western consumers. These are grown in the so-called new agricultural countries (NACs). Sub-Saharan Africa has a comparative advantage in the production of export horticultural commodities, because of its good climatic conditions, geographic proximity to European markets, preferential trade agreements, and, most importantly, an abundance of cheap labour (Barrett et al. 1997).

Agricultural diversification into high-value, labour-intensive commodities such as French beans ('non-traditional' exports) are central to IMF/World Bank programmes to reduce poverty through export-led growth (World Bank 1981, 1995). In particular, agricultural diversification strategies are promoted as a vehicle to enhance gender equity through increased female employment (e.g., Chilean *temporeras* and Mexican *maquiladoras*). Yet research on the social implications of growing non-traditional exports (NTEs) has been largely restricted to Latin America (Collins 1995; Thrupp 1995; Barrientos 1997; Bee and Vogel 1997) with little attention awarded to Africa, where NTEs account for a growing share of women's economic activity. Horticultural exports (principally cut flowers and vegetables) are now the fastest growing agricultural sectors in many African economies (Zimbabwe, Zambia, and Kenya), and a critical source of foreign exchange, particularly with the recent decline in revenues from traditional export crops.

Labour utilization and income distribution

When policy practitioners promote horticultural exports to raise rural incomes, they invariably fail to consider the amount of labour a household must invest to secure a profit. The quality standards that most horticultural crops must meet – governing their texture, fragrance, colour, weight, and shape – make them highly labour-intensive, and resistant to mechanization. Kenya's most widely grown export vegetables – snow peas and French beans – are extremely labour-intensive, demanding 600 and 500 labour days per hectare respectively (Carter et al. 1996; Little 1994). It is mainly women who are compelled to invest more time in specific tasks such as planting and weeding, yet their work remains categorized as unpaid labour. In fact, the economic benefits of growing French beans and other horticultural export crops are predicated upon the unpaid labour of women and children.

Several studies (Schroeder 1996; Carney and Watts 1990; Mackintosh 1989; Mbilinyi 1988) have recorded the cultural norms which govern the division of labour and control of resources between women and men, and which affect the extent to which women can receive benefits from export production. My research confirms that in Meru, biases in men's favour regarding the distribution of land, labour, and income undermine the potential of French bean production to provide developmental benefits for women and children.

First, the exacting labour and time constraints on women involved in export-crop production directly affect their ability to participate in other activities. Women are expected to meet the family's subsistence needs, and to augment household income through the sale of local crops. While men do work on French beans, for the most part they perform tasks of relatively low labour intensity such as clearing fields and applying fertilizer. Furthermore, although men have more spare time to allocate to French bean production than women, there has been no adjustment of the gender division of labour in existing activities between husband and wife. This has eroded women's capacity to fulfil their households' subsistence requirements. Women who are able to retain their proceeds from French bean sales are choosing to allocate more labour to the cultivation of French beans than of subsistence crops. Men resent the withdrawal of female labour from subsistence crops (unless they are given the money earned from the cultivation of the French beans), and have challenged the right of women to use vegetable plots for French bean cultivation. Furthermore, because men are garnering significant amounts of money from export cultivation, they are less likely to work on their wives' plots. As a result, women are compelled to hire labour to perform tasks that were formerly covered by reciprocal labour exchanges.

Second, the gendered nature of property rights also directly affects the benefits women derive from French bean production. In Kenya, women's access to land is mediated by their marital status, their household position, and decisions made about land use by male relatives. As in much of Africa, men have the right to control the proceeds from the crops grown on female plots. Over 33 per cent of the women interviewed claimed that their husbands had either compelled them to grow French beans on their usufruct plots,[1] or retracted their rights to them completely. This violates conjugal norms, because not only are French beans cash crops (the earnings from which traditionally go to men throughout Africa) but they are also vegetable crops (the income from which women have the rights to in customary law).

Third, although French bean production has created a new mechanism for income generation, there is a wide disparity in the distribution of income from it between men and women. My research showed that women perform 72 per cent of the labour for French beans, and obtain 38 per cent of the income. Even where women receive the returns from their labour, they are often compelled to contribute this cash to household expenditures that would, until now, have been their husband's responsibility. Finally, the profitability of French beans has incited men to appropriate the income, which customarily has been under women's control. Conflicts between husbands and wives over the allocation of income from French beans are commonplace and often escalate into household violence. As one female interviewee claimed: 'The crops that result in wife-beating today is coffee and tea, because they are termed as a man's crop. Many husbands misuse money from these crops and when asked they beat their wives. Michiri (French beans) are also cause for beating. When we try to keep our money, our husband asks where it is. If we don't give it to him we are beaten. These crops cause us many problems.'

Because family labour, specifically women's labour, is the fundamental source of labour for French bean production, the success of export horticulture rests on sound cooperation between husband and wife. Traditional social structures which used to deal with marital strife have been eroded, so that women now turn to alternative means of resolving conflict.

Gender and the supernatural

In Meru, the spiritual domain has become the principal area in which gender-based conflicts over crops, property rights, and labour allocation are expressed. Both Christianity and witchcraft reflect the nature of social and economic relations, and hence are useful idioms for interpreting issues of power and domination in rural life. While the presence of witchcraft appears at odds with Christian revivalism, both represent ways of expressing discontent with prevailing social norms, and offer women strategies to reclaim autonomy and security within their households.

Christianity

Africa today cannot be considered apart from the presence of Christianity: a presence which, a couple of generations ago could still be dismissed by some as of marginal importance, and a mere subsidiary aspect of colonialism (Hastings 1990: 208). There are currently over 25 distinct Christian denominations in Central Imenti, 43 churches, and new churches are built each month. Women participate in church groups that meet once a week to practise singing, organize church events, and to discuss both personal and religious matters. While women generally perform duties that replicate their responsibilities at home such as cooking and cleaning, most women I spoke to claimed that they would rather clean the church than their own home, because they were doing it for God, not for their husbands. They told me that they look forward to their weekly gatherings as a time of freedom and an opportunity to gossip, laugh, and seek respite from the routine of daily labour and the problems at home.

The Kenyan state's conception of gender roles is so intertwined with the Christianity proselytised by village leaders that it is nearly impossible to separate Christian values from social life. Young girls are socialized from a very early age to be good Christian girls – obedient, submissive, and accommo-dating – to attract a suitable man for marriage. One interviewee told me that a good woman (*mwekuru umwega* in Kimeru) 'obeys her husband and does not speak rudely to him. She welcomes the guests and does all the work her husband asks her to do.' Her sentiments are widely echoed by other women in Meru, who agree that a *mwekuru umwega* 'does not quarrel with her husband, does not speak badly about her husband and obeys him always'. In fact, some women said that they deserve punishment for failing to meet the Christian standards of a 'good' wife. This linkage between religion and virtue in is reinforced by the Kimeru term *kimatha*, which connotes a bad woman who neglects God, and her husband and children.

Yet despite this, for many women in Meru and elsewhere, the church presents a means to escape the confines of their marriage, since direct chal-lenges to male authority entail too high a cost. In Meru, becoming 'saved' involves witnessing to Christ, and acknowledging Jesus as a personal saviour. The crusade toward being 'born again' has become increasingly widespread through Central Imenti during the last decade. The phenomenon of 'saved' individuals originated among the Methodists and the East African Revivalists in 1947–48 and the numbers continue to rise: my sample of 200 randomly selected households included 95 per cent 'saved' women in comparison to 35 per cent 'saved' men. In fact, I never met a woman who was not 'saved'. In Meru, being born again is now synonymous with being a good Christian and I was encouraged to profess my own conversion, or risk being perceived as an agent of the devil.

Being 'saved' is extremely important to these women: most could recount the moment when they turned over their lives to God. Most women claimed that they have turned to God to bear with the perpetual marital and intra-household struggles they experience; a principal problem is disagreement over French bean income. Many told me that being 'saved' enabled them to handle the difficulties of their marriage; one told me it was 'the only solution' to the powerlessness she experienced in daily life. The transformative power of becoming 'saved' is a significant part of a woman's identity, and offers her not only a means of coping with her life, but also an opportunity to join with other women who share her experience.

Becoming 'saved' is most prevalent among women who have a high stake in the stability of the household system, and few alternatives for autonomy. Women who do not conform to the 'patriarchal bargain'[2] (Kandiyoti 1988) are vulnerable to insecurity, poverty, and landlessness. This is particularly true for women who have no male sons to provide them with land, and thus have no source of protection outside of their marriage.

While female Christian conversion can be seen as capitulation, I view it as a strategy designed to foster self-determination while maintaining an outward appearance of Christian compliance. In order to avoid sanctions from men and the wider community, women act within the parameters of prevailing social norms (von Bulow 1991).

Witchcraft

Witchcraft is not merely a 'traditional relic' of tribal societies, but is woven into the fabric of modern life. Expressions of the occult are well documented in situations of economic change where the introduction of new resources exacerbates social differentiation and increases struggles for power and control (Geschiere 1997; Goheen 1996; Drucker-Brown 1993). Further, theories suggest that women are predominantly associated with the occult because they are marginalized, which is expressed in various symbolic forms such as spirit possession, sorcery and witchcraft (Ardener 1970; Drucker-Brown 1993; Ong 1987).

In Kenya, witchcraft is blamed for illness, death, and natural catastrophe, and people may be lynched and mobbed because of their perceived connections with the occult. Throughout the country, accusations and counter-accusations of witchcraft exacerbate community tensions and contribute to growing violence. In 1994, President Daniel Arap Moi took a stand against occult practices, following reports that devil worshipping and witchcraft were infiltrating educational and government institutions, and widespread claims that his administration was avoiding an investigation because some of its members, as well as opposition figures, were involved in a satanic cult (Wachira 1994). Kenyan politicians are known to exploit people's paranoia by invoking satanism to win votes. For example, during the 1992 elections, a Democratic Party (DP) politician sprinkled a potion in the ballot boxes professing that individuals who failed to vote DP would be haunted by 'the bottle' (*The Nation*, 24 May 1995).

Fear of the occult is pervasive in Meru; witchcraft is inscribed in the consciousness of the area and is expressed in a repertoire of stories, for example: 'I know a girl, Tabitha from Kibirichia, who left home with an unknown woman to be employed by a woman at Maua. But instead of them going to Maua they went to Thika. She was stripped naked and kept in the house. She was told to write a letter home and tell them of her incoming death. She wrote home and the parents received the news with shock. They hurriedly got the police and they saved the girl. The girl later told them of how people were taken there and eaten by other people... That people there were living with the devil'.

In Meru, the changing balance of power between men and women in domestic, economic, and political spheres has led to the emergence of witchcraft accusations by men against women. In the 1920s, colonial administrators had become intent on banishing the issue of witchcraft from Meru, contending that the District's development was being impeded by the persistence of 'superstition', and the perpetuation of 'secret societies'. In particular, officials were concerned over the reports of women's *kiamas* (societies), where women practised witchcraft to ensure the obedience of their husbands. The women's intent was said to be not so much to kill their husbands as 'to force them to seek alternatives, preferably by providing ... gifts sufficient to induce removal of the curse' (Fadiman 1993: 160). A spate of women either giving their husbands *kagweria* – a substance that induces psychosis and leaves control of the household to the wife – or poisoning their husbands to death, was recorded early in this century, and reappeared in the 1970s. *Kagweria*, a liquid taken from certain trees, is mixed with a bouquet of sedative drugs.

Today, women in Meru practise many forms of witchcraft (both sorcery and bewitching)[3] which are widely used to secure power and autonomy within their marriage. *Kagweria* is purchased from knowledgeable women, and its use is rapidly being taught to Meru women by women in other districts. In Githongo Location, a 35-year-old woman administered the potion to her husband, aged 39. The man not only suffered from common dementia as a result, but also experienced a severe psychotic state. Following his hospitalization, his wife was implicated. Under investigation, she disclosed that there was a group of four women who had perfected the recipe and were distributing it to other women. One interviewee described women's involvement in the following way:

'Women buy [*kagweria*] from other women who are old. *Kagweria* is a charm given secretly by women to their men that changes men's mental ability to a worse state. Once a man is fed with *kagweria*, he stops giving orders to his woman and therefore the woman becomes the head of the family. This [use] has increased because we are dealing away with our traditional customs. Before, the clan would intervene in husband and wife cases. Now the clan doesn't do much for us, so we get a solution for ourselves. Men don't respect their wives or they are not all that faithful like before. They still love with other women and this annoys the wives. Most women do not want to accept that a woman should always be under a man, like they tell us. We are envious of the progressing way of other women who have freedom. A way to have freedom is to give *kagweria* … [and obtain] power over the wealth, especially from the good crops.'

One particular interviewee knew of seven cases of bewitching within the last two years, all provoked due to interfamilial struggles over French bean income. Churches regularly organize women's seminars to preach against the practice and to teach women how to ameliorate household struggles through Christian service. Despite this, many of the same women who publicly espouse the tenets of Christianity privately employ witchcraft.

Baraza (public assemblies) are frequently organized by village politicians to mitigate male anxiety regarding women's increased utilization of witchcraft and poisoning, and to lecture women on norms of female obedience. One particular case concerned the poisoning of a village man, whose wife claimed that he refused to allocate any French bean income to her. A village woman described the incident in the following way:

'In *Katheri*, a wife worked with her daughters to bewitch her husband and take all the wealth. The man was forced to stay in the house for three weeks with vomiting and diarrhoea. The church is taking the duty to preach against bewitching now. In June, the Four Square preachers held a crusade and prayed and pointed out one of the women from Kiithe village who has been supplying *kagweria*. They chastised her. But usually these women aren't found because witchcraft can only be carried out at night. It is very secretive... Only talked about... Never seen with the eyes'.

In Meru, Kenya, witchcraft reflects women's struggles for power in an arena in which they have been customarily denied a more direct vehicle for asserting their aims. The growing prevalence of witchcraft is one consequence of the expansion of French bean production and its exacerbating effect on intra-household disparities. As men's individual ambition has overridden their customary social responsibilities (through the appropriation of women's incomes and usufruct rights to land), women have developed strategies to reclaim autonomy and security within their households.

As the number of witchcraft cases in Meru District mounts, men are terrified. The rise in the number of *baraza* and village meetings to lecture women on female obedience is testimony to men's growing fear of female aggression. Men have no reason to believe that their wife will be an exception to the recent movement. As Geschiere contends (1994: 325), 'witchcraft is indeed the dark side of kinship: it reflects the frightening notion that there is hidden aggression and violence where there should be only trust and solidarity'. Thus, as long as men were not jeopardizing women's access to resources in the female domain, women largely allowed public political power to remain in men's hands. But as men have encroached upon the income derived from French beans, a crop culturally coded as female, the boundaries and meanings of gender relationships have changed (Goheen 1996). In this situation, women's resistance cannot be overlooked, because the viability of export-promotion strategies for development depends upon women's willing participation.

It is widely agreed in gender and development circles that an understanding of how resources are distributed within the household is critical to the success of policy interventions (Kabeer 1995; Goetz and Sen Gupta 1994). Yet development practitioners continue to overlook how cultural factors influence the outcome of agricultural diversification initiatives. In this case, the failure to acknowledge cultural dynamics has not only undermined the purported aims of gender equity, but also worsened women's well-being, and ultimately men's security.

Notes

1   Usufruct land is property under male control which women have the rights both to cultivate and to retain the income derived from that production.
2   This phrase refers to women's conformity to social norms – such as being a good wife and mother – in a male-dominated society, in return for rewards such as social acceptance and status.
3   In daily discourse there is little difference between sorcery and witchcraft. In Kiswahili, both are described as *uchawi*, although witches are perceived to have an ascribed status, whereas sorcerers achieve their status through study in the application of substances (Brain 1982).

References

Apter, A. (1993) 'Attinga Revisited: Yoruba Witchcraft and the Cocoa Economy, 1950–1951' in Comaroff, J. and Comaroff, J. (eds) *Modernity and its Malcontents: Ritual and Power in Postcolonial Africa*, University of Chicago Press: Chicago.

Ardener, E. (1970) 'Witchcraft, Economics and the Continuity of Belief' in Douglas, M. (ed) *Witchcraft Confessions and Accusations*, Tavistock: London.

Barrett, H., Browne, A., Ilbery, B., Jackson, G., and Binns, T. (1997) 'Prospects for Horticultural Exports Under Trade Liberalisation in Adjusting African Economies', report submitted to HM Department for International Development.

Barrientos, S. (1997) 'The Hidden Ingredient: Female Labour in Chilean Fruit Exports' in *Bulletin of Latin American Research* 16(1): 71–81.

Bee, A. and Vogel, I. (1997) 'Temporerars and Household Relations: Seasonal Employment in Chile's Agro-Export Sector' in *Bulletin of Latin American Research* 16(1): 83–95.

Brain, J. (1982) 'Witchcraft and Development' in *African Affairs* 81(324): 371–84.

Carney, J. and Watts, M. (1990) 'Manufacturing Dissent: Work, Gender, and the Politics of Meaning in a Peasant Society', *Africa* 60(2): 207–41.

Carter, M., Barnham, B.L., and Mesbah, D. (1996) 'Agricultural Export Booms and the Rural Poor in Chile, Guatemala and Paraguay' in *Latin American Research Review* 31(1): 7–33.

Collins, J. (1995) 'Gender and Cheap Labor in Agriculture', in McMichael, P. (ed) *Food and Agrarian Orders in the World-Economy*, Praeger: Westport.

Drucker-Brown, S. (1993) 'Mamprusi Witchcraft, Subversion and Changing Gender Relations' in *Africa* (63): 531–49.

Fadiman, J. (1993) *When We Began There Were Witchmen, An Oral History from Mt. Kenya*, University of California Press: Berkeley.

Geschiere, P. and Fisiy, C. (1994) 'Domesticating Personal Violence: Witchcraft, Courts and Confessions in Cameroon' in *Africa* 64(3): 323–41.

Geschiere, P. (1997) *The Modernity of Witchcraft*, University of Virginia Press: Charlottesville.

Goetz, A.M. and Sen Gupta, R. (1996) 'Who Take the Credit: Gender, Power and Control over Loan Use in Rural Credit Programmes in Bangladesh' in *World Development* 24(4).

Goheen, M. (1996) *Men Own the Fields: Women Own the Crops: Gender and Power in the Cameroon Grassfields*, University of Wisconsin Press: Madison.

Hastings, A. (1990) 'Christianity in Africa' in King, U. (ed.) *Turning Points in Religious Studies*, T. and T. Clark: Edinburgh.

Kabeer, N. (1995) 'Necessary, Sufficient or Irrelevant? Women, Wages and Intra-household Power Relations in Urban Bangladesh', IDS Working Paper #25, Institute of Development Studies: Brighton.

Kandiyoti, D. (1988) 'Bargaining with Patriarchy' in *Gender and Society* 2(3).

Little, P. (1994) 'Contract Farming and the Development Question' in Little, P. and Watts, M. (eds) *Living Under Contract: Contract Farming and Agrarian Transformation in Sub-Saharan Africa*, University of Wisconsin Press: Madison.

Mackintosh, M. (1989) *Gender, Class and Rural Transition: Agribusiness and the Food Crisis in Senegal*, Zed Books: London.

Mbilinyi, M. (1988) 'Agribusiness and Women Peasants in Tanzania' in *Development and Change* 19(4): 549–83.

Mukhopadhyay, M. (1995) 'Gender Relations, Development Practice and Culture' in *Gender & Development* 3(1), Oxfam GB: Oxford.

Ong, A. (1987) *Spirits of Resistance and Capitalist Discipline: Factory Women in Malaysia*, SUNY Press: Albany.

Schroeder, R. (1996) 'Gone to Second Husbands: Marital Metaphors and Conjugal Contracts in The Gambia's Female Garden Sector' in *Canadian Journal of African Studies* 30(1): 69–87.

Thrupp, L. (1995) *Bittersweet Harvests for Global Supermarkets: Challenges in Latin America's Agricultural Boom*, World Resources Institute: Washington.

von Bulow, D. (1991) 'Transgressing Gender Boundaries: Kipsigis Women in Kenya', CDR Project Paper 91.3, Centre of Development Research: Copenhagen.

Wachira, C., (1994) 'Probe into Devil Worshipping Spawns Controversy', *Interpress Service*, 1 November.

World Bank (1981) 'Towards Accelerated Development in Sub-Saharan Africa', Washington DC.

World Bank (1995) 'Kenya Poverty Assessment', Population and Human Resources Division, Eastern Africa Department, Washington DC.

Acknowledgements

The contributor would like to thank Fulbright, the Social Science Research Council, and the National Science Foundation for their generous support of this research. Appreciation is also extended to the University of North Carolina and the Centre of African Studies, SOAS, for supporting the write-up of this thesis, on which this paper is based.

About the author

Catherine S. Dolan is Lecturer in Marketing, Culture and Society at Green Templeton College, Oxford. She has held Visiting Fellowships at the Centre of African Studies, School of Oriental and African Studies; the Department of Anthropology, University of North Carolina at Chapel Hill; the International Center for Research on Women in Washington, DC; and Boston University's Center for African Studies.

Chapter 8

No time to worship the serpent deities: women, economic change, and religion in north-western Nepal

Rebecca Saul

This chapter first appeared in *Gender & Development* Volume 7, Issue 1, March 1999, p. 31–9

> *Why do the inhabitants of one village in north-western Nepal still follow Buddhist customs, when religious rituals have all but died out in the neighbouring village? Rebecca Saul outlines how the evolution of a competitive tourist economy has affected local social structures and women's roles, as well as women's attitude to the spiritual realm.*

Introduction

This chapter is a tentative exploration of the changing relationships between lay women, and the spiritual realm, in two ethnic Tibetan communities in Barabong in north-western Nepal. It focuses on the ways in which economic and social change has affected women's often unseen and unrecognized spiritual roles within both the household and the community; and on how these roles have in their turn influenced the course of such change. I am drawing on 15 months of doctoral research in Nepal, which set out to look at how individuals in two communities faced, initiated, and resisted change. I found that in the worldview of the inhabitants of Kag and Dzong, the social, physical, and spiritual realms are not distinct, but intricately and inextricably connected.

What is the link between gender and development and this research? First, development interventions are themselves part of a wider process of constant change, and the impact of change, be it the product of 'development', political upheaval, economic re-orientation, or other forces, has related consequences for gender relations within households and communities. The second link is my contention that the Buddhist concept of interconnection – the belief that changes in one realm have a profound impact on the other realms – is, in essence, a concept which should underpin development. Just as Buddhists believe that performing a religious ritual in the physical realm appeases or propitiates a deity in the spiritual realm, so we, as development practitioners and academics, are aware that an irrigation project affects not only agricultural productivity but can also have an impact on the division of labour, land rights, social dynamics, and so on.

Background

Mustang District is located in north-western Nepal, and shares its northern border with Tibet. No motorable roads extend into Mustang but the district capital, Jomsom, can be reached on foot from the city of Pokhara in mid-western Nepal – a five-day walk up into the Kali Gandaki River Gorge – or by a short plane journey. From Jomsom northwards, the local people are described anthropologically as ethnic Tibetans, and within Nepal as Bhote. The people of Baragong in lower Mustang who are the focus of this chapter, speak a local Tibetan dialect (referred to as Southern Mustang Tibetan) and officially follow various Buddhist sects, of which Sakya is currently the predominant one. Marriage practices, social ranking, religious rituals, and general cosmological understandings are similar to those found in areas of Tibet, and among other ethnic Tibetan groups in the Himalayas.

Kag

Kag village has a population of about 360 people in 63 households. It is a minor administrative centre for the area of Baragong, boasting a health post, a police checkpoint, several development offices, and a post office. In addition to all of these 'modern' amenities, a large Buddhist monastery and the remains of an impressive castle suggest that Kag was an important religious, economic, and administrative centre. Today, with a dozen tourist lodges and several camp sites, Kag is one of the most popular tourist destinations for trekkers journeying to and from the Muktinath Valley and north into upper Mustang.

In general, many of the people of Kag village have embraced 'modernization': it was the first village in the area to receive electricity, the first to respond to the arrival of tourists by building guest houses, and also the first village to abandon several of the more important village rituals in Baragong.

Dzong

From Kag, several thousand feet up the Muktinath Valley, lies Dzong village. Dzong is described both by the people who live there, and by other villagers in the area, as a place where the old ways are kept alive. The population of Dzong is slightly smaller than that of Kag, with about 250 inhabitants. Because Dzong is located within a semi- restricted area, tourists can travel to the village for a day, but are not permitted to spend the night there. Dzong does not have a police post, health centre, or post office.

While many of the inhabitants of Dzong participate fully in a market economy, and have embraced the ideology and practice of development along 'modern' lines, Dzong remains – in the words of people in Dzong and other villages in Baragong – 'true to the old ways'. Rituals and practices which have been abandoned in Kag and other villages in the area not only survive in Dzong, but are seen by many Dzongba[1] as the raison d'être of being Dzongba, the things that define them as Dzongba.

Living in Baragong

Like many of the peoples who populate the high mountain regions of Nepal, the Baragongba[2] have a three-pronged subsistence strategy of agriculture, pastoralism, and trade. Kag and Dzong, like most villages in Baragong, are socially stratified. Although there are numerous ways in which the social status of individuals and households can be judged, the main social groupings are those of noble, commoner, and sub-commoner. The middle of these three 'grades' is the most numerous and, in some villages, the only stratum. These hierarchical grades had far more importance in the past than they do today.

In Baragong, as in other ethnic Tibetan societies, there exists an ideal form of household organization which is linked to ideas concerning landholding, inheritance, residence, and marriage, as well as being located in the domains of symbolism and ritual (Phylactou 1989). Although households vary greatly in composition and economic standing, the ideal, and the most common structure for commoners and sub-commoners,[3] is the corporate estate household, called *drongba*. A *drongba* estate is collectively owned by an extended family group. At the core of the *drongba* household is a patriline (group of men related by blood): a man and his wife, or a group of brothers and their wife, the father(s) and mother of the man or brothers, and their children.

Historically, being part of a *drongba* meant high status. *Drongba* households paid tax and performed labour for the noble households, and as a result gained certain privileges, such as first access to irrigation water. *Drongba* households also were the backbone of religious life in the communities of Baragong. Until recently, the wives of male *drongba* heads, called *kimpamo*, had certain rights, including the right to attend the mid-winter festival of *Dokyap*. While noble women rank above all other women in the village including the *kimpamo*, they had no special ritual roles or responsibilities. During the festival, only *kimpamo* women danced the traditional dances in the monastery grounds and the village square. Apart from the obvious honours bestowed upon these women, they were generally more active in village life, and more highly respected than non-*kimpamo* women.

Gender relations

Women in Baragong have significant domestic and civic power. Women are resource-holders – they inherit and own land, and run their own businesses – and decision-makers – they choose their marriage partners, obtain divorces, control their own fertility, and participate in village-level politics.

Marital forms

Baragongba households are ideally based on the Tibetan 'monomarital principle': in each generation of a family, one and only one marriage can be contracted. In theory, the practice of fraternal polyandry (brothers sharing one wife), ensures that the family inheritance is kept within one household, since all the sons remain in the household into which they were born and share the inheritance, rather than allowing inheritance by one child only. If there are no sons, a daughter inherits the estate and brings her husband into the household; it is also possible, but quite rare, for her to marry polygynously, to share a husband with her younger sister or sisters. Although her husband is seen as a male household head, it is the woman who is recognized as the estate holder. In practice, Baragongba women who inherit their own patrimonial estate have more say in household affairs than those who share their husbands' patrimony.

Decision-making in the household

The household in Baragong is a corporate unit. All money, land, and household goods (except dowry goods, which are the wife's property) are jointly owned by the husband(s) and wife. Husbands should not dispose of property without their wives' consent; nor should wives without their husbands'. Couples who are apart because of business make independent day-to-day decisions. According to couples interviewed (and my own observations confirmed this), power relations between husband and wife are relatively equally balanced. Couples stated that this depended more on personality than gender. The ideal is for disputes to be talked through, and a solution agreed upon mutually. Indeed, the power of the head of household is narrowly limited: all household members – even the children – are involved in forming opinions and in executing decisions. While the eldest brother still has the highest status in the home and the community as household head, within the household he cannot overrule unilaterally the wishes of any other household member (see Levine 1980: 287).

Gender division of labour

The division of labour between the sexes is generally relaxed: both men and women farm, herd, trade, and practise business. Women tend to work harder than men, however, as they have primary responsibility for running the household, cooking, collecting water and firewood, looking after children, and performing many of the more laborious agricultural tasks such as weeding and processing grain. There are few hard-and-fast rules, however, and each household manages its workload differently, depending on its labour resources.

However, it is true that, as a result of their relatively heavier domestic workload, women tend to have fewer social responsibilities outside the home. Women often told me that because meetings are called at night they cannot attend – they must cook the evening meal and care for small children.

Similarly, meetings in distant villages are difficult for them to attend because of child-care and domestic responsibilities. It is usually men who attend meetings as representatives of their households, and it is men who hold the positions of 'headman' and 'assistant headman' in the village. With the integration of Baragong into the political system of Nepal, men's political roles have been strengthened; women rarely hold positions of power on the new 'village development committees' (VDCs) or at the district level.

Spirituality and the changing role of women

In Baragong, women have always been integral to the spiritual maintenance of the household and the community. However, while women in the village of Dzong continue to play an important part in the spiritual life of their house-holds and the community, the importance of women's spiritual role in Kag has diminished. Why this difference between the two communities? In order to answer this question, we must look more closely at how the lives of women in Kag and Dzong differ. I will discuss three major changes to women's roles and status brought about by changes in land-holding, tourism, and development.

Land-holding

First, and perhaps most importantly, the system of *drongba* estates in Kag was disbanded several years ago. This means that all people within the village have the same rights and responsibilities. There are no ritual roles, or political offices, that are open only to heads of *drongba* households. In Dzong, however, the titles of *chuktwa* (male household head) and *kimpano* still exist, and ritual, though not administrative, importance is attached to them. Men from all households in Dzong can hold the offices of headman and assistant headman, but only male and female heads of estate-holding households can participate in certain religious festivals and retreats, such as *Dokyap*.

In Kag, disbanding the *drongba* estates has meant that *kimpamo* women play a greatly reduced role in the ritual life of the village. When they do participate, they often do so alongside women from households which, in the past, were not *drongba* households. Former *kimpamo* told me that they see their ritual labour as a burden which keeps them from other, more prestigious economic activities, rather than as an honour bestowed upon them because of their status. These other, more lucrative, economic activities are tourism and other income-generating activities.

The impact of tourism

Baragong was opened to foreign trekkers in 1974. By the late 1980s, it was attracting more than 30,000 tourists every year. In Kag, tourism is an important part of the village economy; in comparison, Dzong has no tourist economy. While tourists visit year-round, the peak period – September to November

– coincides with the harvesting and processing of buckwheat and the planting of barley and wheat, as well as with the large regional harvest festival held in Muktinath. The second most popular time to trek in the Annapurna region is in the spring: a time of reunion, local archery festivals, communal work, and preparation for the harvest. Running a tourist lodge denies the household the labour of at least one member during periods when their contribution is most needed, and further limits both the social and spiritual roles of these household members.

The first tourist lodge in Kag was built in 1976; by 1995 there were ten, and a further two planned. It is primarily women who run lodges. Male and female lodge-owners cited several reasons for this: cooking, cleaning, and hospitality are tasks typically taken on by women, and thus local people feel that women are naturally more capable of running lodges. Second, it is generally women who stay in the village year-round, and hence they tend to take on the primary responsibility for the least seasonal economic activities. Third, women are judged able to look after small children and run lodges simultaneously.

However, women who run lodges have less free time to engage in community rituals, festivals, and monastic retreats. Pema Dolkar, a woman lodge-owner in Kag, complained that she often 'felt like a prisoner' in her own home: 'I would like to go to Yartung [a harvest festival in the neighbouring community of Muktinath] in the autumn, but I have not been now for five years because there have been so many trekkers. Sometimes it is so busy that I cannot even go to Tse chu [a village ritual on the tenth day of each month] and have to send someone else from the household instead' (personal communication, 1995).

While many female lodge-owners find that their movements beyond the village are restricted, tourism and business have both enabled and encouraged men (and non-lodge-owning women) to spend longer periods away from the village. Whereas in the past women played an important role in both regional trade and the salt-grain trade between Nepal and Tibet, women who have the responsibility of running a lodge rarely participate in business outside of the village.

Women who run lodges also tend to visit other households in the village less often, and participate less in the sharing of food which is so common between kin, neighbours, and friends. While it is still customary for lodge-owners to offer tea to neighbours and friends without charge, the sharing of vegetables and other desirable foods now bypasses the lodges. As one woman, whose female cousin runs a lodge, commented: 'Why would my sister [cousin] give spinach to me when she could sell it to the tourists for money? We used to share food between our households all the time here [in Kag], but now many people keep things to themselves so that they can make money.'

People also say that the Buddhist ethic of hospitality has suffered since the advent of tourism. The following tale, told throughout Baragong, illustrates this point. 'There was a woman who set up a travellers' rest house a little way up the Thorong La [a frequently travelled pass between Baragong and the neighbouring district of Manang]. She knew that people coming from

Manang, tourists and locals, would be thirsty and need a drink so it was a good business idea. But this woman – man kalo cha! [black soul or heart] – she would not even give away one glass of water. Local people should always receive one glass of tea free, even in a lodge; but she would even charge for water! She was very greedy and made much money. After she died, about two or three years ago, her soul did not find the path [to 'heaven', where souls are weighed to determine their next incarnation]. She still wanders this world, haunting and possessing people. She has possessed [a certain woman from Dzong], as well as Baragongba in Kathmandu and Assam' (personal communication, 1996).

The impact of 'development'

With the opening of Baragong to tourists, 'development' was not far behind. Development ideology and practice in Kag and Dzong have proceeded in very different directions. Villagers in both communities have radically different views of what development is and should be at the village level.

There are stories of failed projects and lack of local participation in Kag. I heard divergent views of development between the younger and older generations. While younger people adhere to the bottom-up model of development held in Dzong, older people in Kag are oriented towards dependence on the outside. This idea of development as a top-down redistribution of resources from the state, sees development as a gift which 'has or has not come' and the role of villagers as passive recipients in this process (Clarke undated). One woman in Kag stated: 'I do not know the names of any of the development projects here, only the police office and the office that my son works with [ACAP]. I don't know what he does, something with trees... Some office people came and planted some trees, but no one has watered them and most have died. ... I don't know what will happen to the trees after they have grown, whether the development people will sell them, or whether they will even be used by the Kagpa... Up to now, ACAP has done nothing but make garbage tips. They make tourists sign their names when they arrive in Kag'. Some of the accountability for failed projects must, of course, lie with the development projects themselves.

One old Kagpa woman expressed the dissonance between old ideas of 'goodness' and the ideas held by those who wish to bring development to the village: 'In the old days, we used to drink water right out of the Dzong River. The water out of the river is very good for you. Some people still drink from it [even though there is a clean water project]. We old people say that walking through the river makes the water *choko* [clean], not *jutho* [polluted]. We did not hear that the river water was bad for us before the Nepalis and development came! Mountain water is colder and tastier.'

Many Kagpa feel that development in their village has a bad track record because people are too busy with their own work and there are too many poor people: 'If there was enough money in the village, people could cooperate and do their own development.' Many of the meetings called by project staff to discuss the village's future development were attended only by lodge-owners; non-lodge-owners said they felt that development was for tourists, rather than for villagers. According to NGO staff, this low level of interest has led to many projects pulling out of Kag. During group discussions, interviews, and in casual conversations, villagers listed a number of reasons for this lack of interest in development projects. Lodge-owners rarely cooperate with each other, and because of their high social and economic status, few other villagers are willing to participate in community projects. Those who had enough money to install solar power for showers do not want electricity for the whole village, because then all lodges would be able to provide hot showers. Tourism has furthered competition rather than cooperation, especially between lodge-owners. Competition for tourist money is evident when one passes the painted rocks along the trail leading to Kag, announcing that this lodge or that lodge has a hot shower, the tastiest apple pie, the best views.

Because most lodge-owners are women, the main conflicts are between them rather than men. The fact that gender and development literature and practice has paid much attention to women's cooperative development efforts may mean that the lack of cooperation in Kag is more noticeable than similar behaviour would be on the part of men.

Unlike the highly competitive market of tourism, business ventures in Dzong, especially those which require villagers to travel further afield to East Asia, often require the labour and financial resources of several households working together. Because of their relative isolation, and the lack of a tourist economy, the people of Dzong have had to seek support from government agencies and NGOs to improve life in the village; a key element of this relationship is that they also show commitment in the form of labour and other inputs into the projects. 'Our own village, we must build ourselves' is the development slogan heard throughout Nepal. (In the past, labour obligations were fulfilled by *drongba* households only. This has been a powerful catalyst for changing the *drongba* system to limit it to ritual activities, rather than political and economic ones.) The villagers have often worked with the people of their neighbouring villages Chongkhor and Putak in order to attract expertise, materials, and money for their projects. In sum, the Dzongba seem to have been relatively successful in making development work for them, without losing control over important village decisions; the moral ideology of equity and a commitment to 'community' have been strengthened in Dzong.

When the Dzong villagers decide that a project is needed, the village leaders sit down with the headmaster (who writes Nepali) and draft a letter to the appropriate agency. Several projects applied for in this manner have now been completed. For example, Dzong is supplied with limited electricity in the winter months by a hydro-electric project supported by the government of Nepal. Numerous small projects which the villagers initiated have been carried out with the help of development funds, including the construction of a new mill. CARE agreed to supply the necessary materials; the labour was supplied by all households.

Lay women and their spiritual roles

People's relationships with the spiritual realm are influenced by social, economic, and political change. In particular, the changing economic role of women in Kag has had profound effects on their role in religious practice.

Caring for the lu

Lu are serpent spirits which, when pleased, bring wealth and prosperity, and when angered, bring illness and misfortune.[4] Daily rituals of offering food and burning incense are enacted to propitiate the household *lu*; these are almost exclusively performed by household women. The differences in household rituals enacted in Dzong and Kag reflect what is perceived as necessary for the prosperity of the household. In Dzong, daily offerings to the serpent deities are still viewed as a vitally important part of household ritual, appeasing potentially harmful serpent deities and enlisting their aid, while in Kag prosperity is seen as less dependent on the *lu*. My Dzong landlady explained that '[I]f the *lu* ritual is not done the household will become poor, sick, and inharmonious. It will be a "dirty house".' However, in contrast, many houses in Kag do not worship *lu* or perform rituals for them any longer. A significant number of households in Kag give offerings only once a week rather than daily, as is recommended by monks and devout villagers alike. During the winter, many women in Kag do not feed the *lu* at all; they claim that the *lu* are sleeping, and therefore do not need to be appeased. This is convenient for women who leave the village during the winter for sunnier climes.

Celebrating Dokyap

The ceremony of *Dokyap* is intended to enlist the aid of benevolent Buddhist divinities and regional gods and goddesses in the protection of the village. A grandmother in Dzong told me: 'The performance of *Dokyap* pleases God. It keeps sickness and death away from people and livestock. It ensures good harvests and stops torrential rain and wind storms. For the welfare of the village, *Dokyap* must be done'.

Historically, *Dokyap* has been an extremely important event for the political and religious unity of the area and the hegemony of the local ruling class. While in Dzong the ritual has survived to this day, in Kag it declined and eventually died several decades ago.

In Dzong, *Dokyap* is still an important event: large fines are imposed on male and female *drongba* household heads who are absent from the village or who fail to participate in any of the events during the seven-day ritual. Villagers consider the festival vitally important for the preservation of local culture, the accumulation of religious merit, the expulsion of evil, and the social unity of the village.

Each day, at noon, a large drum calls the female heads of *drongba* households away from their drinking party in a house near the monastery (village women take turns hosting the party each year). Everyone gathers in the village square where the women sing and dance in traditional lines. Only women born or married into Dzong can participate; single women and widows are excluded. All of the women wear *shuli*, the ceremonial head-dresses which mark them as married heads of commoner estate-holding households.

The songs sung by the women are vitally important for the efficacy of the exorcism ritual; the women singers carry the ritual effigies, and lead the procession of villagers to the monastery and to the far reaches of the village. Four masked young men chase and beat the women if they do not sing loud enough, ordering them to 'sing for the protection of the village'. The seven *Dokyap* songs can only be taught by women, and only then; they must never be sung at any other time, and should not be revealed to outsiders.

The events which preceded and followed the cessation of Kag's *Dokyap* reveal much about the importance of women in maintaining the community's spirituality, and about how and why these roles have changed. A host of social and political tensions contributed to the dissolution of *Dokyap* in Kag, and this is still the cause of much discussion and tension within the village.

The first version of events that I heard was told by a noblewoman in Kag, who has a good knowledge of history but also a vendetta against the man she names as the villain in the scenario. '*Dokyap* stopped in Kag 22 years ago, when Dhundup [not his real name] was the big man. He had two wives. His first wife wanted to leave him so she arranged for her younger sister to marry him. At this time, when he took his new wife, they did not like the *Dokyap* because we [the nobles] did. We loved it, so they went against it just out of spite ... and maybe because they were embarrassed about the family situation'. The idea that Kag's *Dokyap* stressed the divisions between nobles, commoners, and sub-commoners was confirmed as part of the reason why many commoners in Kag ceased to participate; villagers said that they 'did not want to beg for food from the nobles' and that 'dancing for food and drink was degrading'.

Another reason given for the decline of the ritual is the rise of economic development. As economic considerations for many villagers have begun to outweigh cultural or religious ones, people travel south in greater numbers during the winter, and thus are absent during *Dokyap*. Rice and barley, the staple foods of the festival, have begun to be seen as cash commodities: why contribute as much as 63 pounds of rice and barley (the contribution of a large household for the entire festival), when that grain could be sold for a profit? In addition, many ceremonial head-dresses used for *Dokyap* were sold to tourists in the 1970s, and the cash invested in lodges and other business ventures.

This also reveals a shift in perceptions of status. In the past, a woman who wore a particularly beautiful and richly adorned head-dress conferred status on her household. To sell a head-dress in the 1920s or 1940s would have been unthinkable, since a commoner woman without one had no real status and could not participate in communal ritual events. As modern clothing and consumer goods have replaced local dress and jewellery as signs of household prosperity, many family heirlooms have been sold.

The cessation of *Dokyap* in Kag has obvious religious implications. Singing the traditional songs is an important part of communal cleansing and accumulation of merit. In Dzong, this is still seen as so important that female heads of household who are absent from the village during *Dokyap* (usually because they have travelled south for the winter and are unable to return because of illness or heavy snows) pay a large fine, and are forbidden to participate in the ritual the following year, causing great shame for a household. In Kag, this is not the case.

Conclusion

Few Kagba women of the younger generation wish the ritual of *Dokyap* to be revived, and many of the old songs have been forgotten. What are the implications of the changes in religious observation and in economic activity in these communities for women, and for development policy and practice? A broad analysis of women's roles and women's work is needed, which includes spiritual roles and responsibilities. Do development researchers and workers include all dimensions of women's work in their information-gathering and policy formulation? Do they recognize women's 'unseen' spiritual maintenance roles within their communities, which could be enhanced or undermined by development? How do women's spiritual, reproductive, productive, and community roles support (or weaken) each other? Most importantly – and this is certainly not the first time that this question has been asked – are 'economic development' and 'purchasing power' the only yardsticks by which household and community well-being should be measured?

Kag women who run lodges and spend many months away from the village are perceived by others to have neglected their social, and hence spiritual, obligations. Women's cooperative groups (so common among ethnic Tibetans in Nepal), and the practice of sharing household resources among neighbours, friends, and kinswomen, have virtually ceased in Kag. As the story of the dead lodge-owner whose soul wanders this earth illustrates, economic and social changes have consequences for the spiritual life of the Baragongba. Although the Dzongba are as successful in business as the Kagpa, and indeed travel abroad more frequently, they still consider it vitally important to be a participating member of the village. Sharing food, labour, and goods between households reinforces village solidarity, and expresses local ideas of morality and social obligations. Full social and physical participation in village life also maintains spiritual harmony within the village. Dzongba women do not seem to feel the same conflicts as Kagpa women.

For women in Kag today, there are 'paradoxes, conflicts and ambivalence surrounding the apparent contradiction between enduring religious values and current trade practice, between those who aspire toward indigenous (Buddhist) notions of "goodness" and those whose imaginings lean toward the glamour of "life in the fast lane"'(Watkins 1996: 6). The negative impact on individuals and the community of Kag women's neglect of traditional social and spiritual responsibilities should be weighed against the possible benefits to individual women, their households, and to women's collective status in the community of increased female economic contributions to their households. Women are gaining respect for their business acumen and their ability to earn money. My research assistant in Dzong, Khandro, offers an excellent example. In the first year of her marriage, her parents-in-law wanted Khandro to stay in the village, but her husband encouraged her to accompany him on a business trip. He stated to family and friends that 'she [his wife] is very clever and will be of great help to me in business. Why would I marry a woman who had no head for business?' The qualities of independence and individualism are becoming more prized; however, the older generation mourn the loss of social cohesion and community spirit.

Notes

1   People of Dzong
2   People of Barabong
3   Noble households were excluded from the *drongba* system, as it was they in the past who benefited from it.
4   The beliefs of the Baragongba about where the *lu* live and how they must be treated translate into practical rules concerning hygiene and health, as well as rules which protect the environment (Mumford 1989).

References

Clarke, G. (undated) 'Development (Vikas) in Nepal: Mana from Heaven', draft paper prepared for the Asian Studies Association Fourth Decennial Conference, Oxford.

Levine, N. (1980) 'Nyinba polyandry and the allocation of paternity' in *Journal of Comparative Family Studies* 11(3).

Mumford, S.R. (1989) *Himalayan Dialogue: Tibetan Lamas and Gurung Shamans in Nepal*, University of Wisconsin Press: Madison.

Phylactou, M. (1989) *Household Organisation and Marriage in Ladakh – Nepal Himalaya*, unpublished PhD thesis, London School of Economics and Political Science.

Watkins, J.C. (1996) *Spirited Women: Gender, Women and Cultural Identity in the Nepal Himalaya*, Columbia University Press: New York.

About the author

Rebecca Saul works for CARE International UK as a programme officer for South Asia and Latin America. She lived in Nepal for three years conducting research and working as a consultant, and has a PhD in social anthropology.

Chapter 9

A double-edged sword: challenging women's oppression within Muslim society in Northern Nigeria

Fatima L. Adamu

This chapter first appeared in *Gender & Development* Volume 7, Issue 1, March 1999, p. 56–91

Islamic development NGOs find it difficult enough to finance their work, because Western donors are often reluctant to sponsor NGOs with religious affiliations. Muslim women activists working to achieve development with gender equity face an even greater challenge: they must secure funding as well as justify their goals to those within their societies who see feminism as a threat.

Until recently, there has been a muted relationship between 'gender and development' and religion, in spite of the importance of religion in the lives of many women who are the beneficiaries of gender and development (GAD) programmes. As a Muslim woman activist involved in work on gender issues in Northern Nigeria, I consider the issue of religion to be particularly relevant to the policy and practice of GAD in Muslim societies. Because gender issues are both religious and political concerns in many Muslim societies (Hale 1997; Mernissi 1996), any attempt to reform gender relations that excludes religion is likely to fail.

Currently, Muslim women in many communities throughout the world are re-defining Islam as a legitimate tool for engaging with and tackling gender issues in Muslim societies (Baden 1992). It is true that interpretations of Islam have been used by leaders in the past, and are still used today, as grounds for refusing women their rights as individuals, including access to secular, 'Western' education and the right to participate equally in politics (Callaway and Creevey 1994). In Nigeria, women's right to be elected to the secular central government is being challenged in the name of Islam. Consequently, Hausa women of Muslim faith in Northern Nigeria are being left far behind, compared with their sisters from the South (ibid.).

Nigeria is a secular state, but the majority of the population in Northern Nigeria are Muslims. The Hausa people are the dominant ethnic group in the region. It is estimated that Hausa is the largest ethnic group in Africa, with a population of 50–60 million (Furniss 1996). Islam reached Northern Nigeria via trans-Saharan trade routes, about the eleventh and twelfth century. By the nineteenth century, Islam had become part of the cultural identity of the Hausa (Imam 1991). The impact of Islam on Hausa society was deep and wide-spread, and it is difficult to separate the two cultures: the Jihad movements of the early nineteenth century, which aimed to 'purify' Islam and prevent it mixing with indigenous traditional beliefs, had a far- reaching impact on Northern Nigeria.

Few attempt to underplay the centrality of Islam in determining the position of women in Muslim societies, and its impact on the everyday lives of women. In such societies, ideas about gender relations are derived from interpretations of Islam, and these ideas are enacted either through legislation or public opinion. Matters of central concern to women such as inheritance, marriage, child custody, divorce, and other marital relationships are governed by Islamic rules in many Muslim societies. In Northern Nigeria, the Shari'ah courts, which practise Islamic personal law, remain the most relevant and widely used legal system, despite the option of using the civil court. Legal matters which concern women in their role as wives and mothers – for example, disputes over inheritance, marriage, divorce, and child custody – are therefore commonly conducted or resolved within the Islamic legal system rather than the parallel Nigerian civil legal system.

In questioning such issues, Muslim feminists have found themselves in the middle of a conflict between Islam and the 'West', facing a double-edged sword. The importance and relevance of women's participation in the Islamic movement, and the emergence of Islamic women's movements in the Muslim world, have been interpreted by some as 'an ambiguous political struggle', where women are on the one hand 'fighting actively against their inequality, but on the other [are] accepting or supporting their own subordination' (Duval 1997: 39). But despite conflicting interpretations of our struggle, the fact of the matter is that Muslim women activists are confronting issues of concern to the generality of Muslim women; and we are doing so in our own way. This chapter is my personal reflection on this struggle. What are the consequences for women who attempt to reform gender relations in Muslim societies? What problems do we encounter, and how do they relate to the ideas, plans, and programmes of GAD?

GAD, Islam, and the West

GAD can be seen as a battlefield in which the conflict between Islam and the West is played out in Muslim societies. While much writing on women and development in Muslim societies from Western academic researchers and media commentators shows a lack of understanding and bias (Callaway and Creevey 1994; Toynbee 1997), GAD is viewed with suspicion by some Muslim scholars as offering a means to the West to wipe out the values and beliefs of Muslim societies. Some Western writers do indeed suggest that Muslim women may be used to attack Islam and undermine Islamic values. Mervyn Hiskett, for example – a British scholar who has spent years in Northern Nigeria and who has written on how to deal with the expansion of Islam in the West – describes women as 'Islam's Achilles' heel'; his solution is the assimilation of Muslim women into 'Western' culture (Faruqi 1994).

Bugaje, a Nigerian Islamic scholar, who is a liberal on gender issues, echoed these suspicions in his 1997 discussion of women's empowerment: 'these two decades, during which the UN championed the globalization of women's issues, happened to be the two decades during which the UN became increasingly a tool in the hands of a few Western nations who were using it to achieve their selfish political goals. ... This left many Muslims unsure about the role of the UN in respect of women's issues' (Bugaje 1997: 9). While I would wish to challenge such general suspicions on the part of Muslim scholars, they are borne out to some extent by certain UN documents dealing with women, which emphasize individual rights more than responsibilities and community rights. Moreover, the incompatibility of the documents with some Islamic values – especially regarding inheritance law, moral values and practice, and the role and nature of the family – is apparent. For instance, Article 15.4 of the UN Convention on the Elimination of all Forms of Discrimination Against Women (CEDAW) says: 'States Parties shall accord to men and to women the same rights with regard to the law relating to the movement of persons and the freedom to choose their residence and domicile'. While this may seem reasonable, problems arise in practice for Muslim women, since it is incompatible with Islamic ideas of household relations, and the division of responsibility between husband and wife. Once a marriage contract is fully concluded and enacted, it is the husband's responsibility to provide the material and sexual needs of his wife. In return, the movements and activities of the wife outside the household need the consent of the husband. In Hausa society, the principle of male responsibility for maintenance is reinforced by the fact that it is seen as socially appropriate for a wife to seek divorce if her husband fails to support her. Records from courts in Sokoto from 1988 to 1998 show that 53 per cent of the civil cases brought before the court (not all of which are concerned with divorce) are maintenance-related.

Other principles adopted in international documents carry similar messages. In the Forward-Looking Strategies for the Advancement of Women, agreed at the Third World Conference on Women in Nairobi in 1991, the 50th paragraph agrees that women should have equal rights with men in matters of inheritance. This is incompatible with the Islamic law of inheritance, which gives women half of what men inherit due to the laws regarding men's responsibility to maintain women.

Moreover, UN documents do not recognize the abuse of women's economic rights inherent within the current Western development model. They therefore fail as an instrument for Muslim women to use in fighting the mismanagement and exploitation of resources in the developing world, both by the elites within those societies, and those in the West.

The practical implications of ignoring Islam for GAD work

Even if such suspicions are unfounded, and GAD programmes are not in prin-ciple intended to undermine Islamic values, the exclusion of religion from development discourse and practice is in itself Western in orientation, and contrary to Islamic principle. Perhaps more importantly, it is unrealistic. The lives of women in many Muslim societies, including those of Northern Nigeria, challenge the idea of considering gender issues separately from religion: Islam is not just a religion to which we claim allegiance, or which we mark through performing rituals. It is a total way of life, and we aspire to conduct our lives according to its teachings. In her study of the influence of Islam and Western education on women in Sokoto, northern Nigeria, Knipp (1987) identifies three categories of women: non-Western-educated women, young women, and professional women. Some of their words are presented here.

A non-Western-educated woman says: 'Islam is a great influence on what I say and do, what my relation is supposed to be with my husband, my family[1] and my children' (ibid.: 407). Another woman explains: 'Most things that you do in life are guided by the religion: whatever you do, you do for God's sake. ... Islam is my religion ... it guides one as to how he's going to lead his life' (ibid.: 139–40). A young university student says that 'every single thing, how to enter a toilet, how to stay with others, how to acquire knowledge, everything is in the Qur'an ... personally, to me, Qur'an is everything' (ibid.: 277). One professional women states: 'Islam is a way of life, not a part of life; whatever I do, I hope it conforms with the religion, so more or less all my behaviour, all my acts, I'm praying they conform with the religion. It is more or less my own way of life' (ibid.: 406). It can be seen from these words that any GAD initiative which is based on the idea of a separation between women's religious and gender identities will risk alienating and excluding many Muslim women.

An example from my own experience of an initiative which tried to operate in this way is the Family Economic Advancement Programme (FEAP), part of the Nigerian government's poverty-alleviation programme. Since 1996, the government has designated millions of US dollars to assist women with credit to improve their income-generation activities. In order to receive this credit, people are required to form cooperative societies. By this condition, those Muslim women in the north who practise purdah (seclusion) are excluded. In 1998, when I was conducting research in Sokoto state, northern Nigeria, many Muslim women in this situation asked me to assist them in forming cooperative societies, in order to meet the credit requirement. The volume of such requests overwhelmed me; I contacted the relevant authorities about this matter, and they promised to look into the case. We started to discuss the idea of getting around the problem of seclusion by forming a cooperative society within an extended or polygynous household (which is the dominant house-hold form in this area). This idea would depend on whether women wished to work with each other in this way within a household; it would also involve visiting individual households in order to make them aware of the opportunity to gain access to credit, in addition to discussing the usual difficulties and problems that may arise. I left the country to study abroad shortly afterwards, and do not yet know the outcome of the discussion and the authority's final decision. If my research had not coincided with the implementation of FEAP, these women might have been overlooked, as was the case with other women's development programmes.

Many GAD programmes are substantially funded by international funding organizations, the majority of which are from Western societies. For Muslim women activists, who need money to fund our programmes, this presents a challenge: we must strike a balance between meeting the requirements of the funding organizations and carrying out our work, as well as balancing this with the opposition we encounter from some quarters of our societies. This is an enormous and difficult task; at the centre of it is our concern for the condition of the women with whom we are working.

'Partnership', donors, and religious NGOs

My concern as a Muslim gender activist has increased in the course of interaction with some funding organizations. Much has been said about the idea of 'partnership' between donors and local NGOs. Although it is an improvement upon the previous relationship between donors and NGOs, we still need to make progress. The organizations and sectors of work which are successful in attaining funding are still chosen almost exclusively by the donors, who define their areas of interest, while local NGOs struggle to fit in. In desperate need of money, some NGOs re-adjust their areas of interest to accommodate the donors' interest, even if this means their work is less useful in responding to the pressing areas of need in the community.

In the 1980s, my experience was that many funding organizations chose not to work with Islamic women's organizations because of their religious orientation. Although this has changed somewhat, this reluctance still resurfaces regularly when interacting with some of them. For example, in March 1998 I attended a workshop on capacity-building and possible partnerships for northern Nigerian NGOs, as part of a project run by the British government's Department for International Development (DFID).[2] When the NGOs were divided into groups, according to the workshop methodology, a disagreement erupted over a request from some participants that there should be a group of religious NGOs (some of us were representing Islamic and Christian organizations). Those opposed to our being grouped together argued that we had been invited not because of our religious affiliations, but in our capacity as NGOs involved with women's development initiatives. We wanted to know what was wrong with being a religious NGO, and who should define the identity of NGOs – themselves, or funders? Do NGOs with a firm rooting in a religion have to appear to change their identity in order to satisfy the donors?

Even after an area of work is mutually identified by a donor and a local NGO which is based on religion, and after funding is agreed, other problems concerned with the issue of religion may arise in the implementation. For instance, in 1994, the director of a US-based funding organization visited the state where I worked, in search of NGOs with whom to work. During his visit, he made a presentation to representatives of different NGOs on the areas of work for which funding would be provided. Our NGO looked at the areas and – although we were not comfortable with some components in many of them – in consideration of our local needs, we decided to collaborate with the donor in the area of health care. One of the uncomfortable aspects of this area was the funder's expectation that we would integrate a family-planning component. Our NGO's stand on the issue has been that family-planning is a private affair, with no imposition from any organization or authority. We duly expressed our concern to the funders, and a consensus was reached in principle. However, in practice it was a challenge to work with the donor because the project, consisting of all the components that the donor expected to see, and its funding, operated as one system; as one part was affected, so also were the others.

While we were having difficulties in dealing with the funding organization, we had to face another problem of opposition and resentment from the community in which we were working. In particular, the presence of a vehicle that belonged to an American funding organization on our organization's premises was misinterpreted by visitors as an indication that we might be bought or used by the USA against Islam.

Lessons and conclusion

In my experience, few women or men in Muslim communities disagree with the content of GAD programmes which address women's practical needs and interests, or even the reform of gender relations, aiming for a fairer society. However, many question GAD programmes on principle, viewing them as illegitimate because they are 'Western'. In line with this, Muslim women activists, including myself, may be branded Western agents, funded by foreign powers to undermine Islam. As a result of this attitude, and funders' mistrust of organizations which have a religious affiliation, the concerns of Muslim women remain unacknowledged and unaddressed. As it is said, 'when two elephants fight, it is the grass that suffers'.

A weakness of many so-called 'gender and development' programmes is that by targeting women and women's issues only, and by excluding men and other issues of wider social interest from the gender/development discourse and practice, an impression is created that women are the only sex vulnerable to Western influence. In my experience, this may increase Muslim communities' suspicion about what 'gender issues' mean, and harden their stand against interventions which promote women's interests and needs. Focusing on women's rights is seen as a means of diverting attention from the pressing economic and political problems facing many members of Muslim societies, especially in the South and East. Not only are international economic and political bodies involved in this, but local elites are also implicated. In the name of preserving 'tradition', they use the issue of women and the debate about women's rights to legitimize their position, and to divert the attention of ordinary people from the soaring unemployment and political oppression that characterize their lives.

Finally, the difficult and fragile relationship between Islamic women's organizations and international donor organizations, which are predominately from Western societies with a Christian heritage, perpetuates the marginalization of Muslim women activists in the transformation of their society and religion. Since, as I have discussed, Islam is a religion which embraces all aspects of Muslim women's lives, and shapes their experiences, any GAD initiative that attempts to exclude religious concerns from its planning or implementation is likely to exclude Muslim women, and to record a low level of success in addressing their practical needs and long-term interests.

Notes

1   When a Hausa woman says 'family', she is referring to her parents' family, not her marital family, hence the reference to 'husband and my children' as different from 'my family'.
2   The theme of the workshop was 'Capacity Building for Decentralized Development'. It took place in Kano, 10–12 February 1998.

References

Afshar, H. (1998) *Islam and Feminism: An Iranian Case-Study*, Basingstoke and London: Macmillan Press Ltd.
Baden, S. (1992) *The Position of Women In Islamic Countries – Possibilities, Constraints and Strategies for Change*, Briefing on Development and Gender, Report No. 4, prepared for special programme, WID, Netherlands Ministry of Foreign Affairs (DGIS), 1994.
Bugaje, U. (1997) 'Women's empowerment and Islam', paper presented at a symposium on Islam and contemporary issues, organized by the Movement for Islamic Culture and Awareness, Nigeria.
Callaway, B. and Creevey, L. (1994) *The Heritage of Islam, Women, Religion and Politics in West Africa*, Lynne Rienner Publishers: London.
Duval, S. (1997) 'New veils and new voices: Islamist women's groups in Egypt' in Ask, K. and Tjomsland, M. (eds) *Women and Islamisation – Carving a New Space in Muslim Societies*, Chr. Michelsen Institute report series No. 3.
Faruqi, M.H. (1994) 'Turning xenophobia into social policy', a review of *Some to Mecca Turn to Pray: Islamic Values in the Modern World* by M. Hiskett (The Claridges Press) in *Impact International* 24(3).
Furniss, G. (1996) Poetry, Prose and Popular Culture in Hausa. Washington: Smithsonian; Edinburgh: EUP; Ibadan: IUP.
Hale, S. (1997) *Gender Politics in Sudan: Islamism Socialism and the State*,

Westview Press: Boulder.

Imam, A.M. (1991) 'The Development of Women's Seclusion in Hausaland, Northern Nigeria: Women Living Under Muslim Laws,' *Dossier*   9/10: 4–18.

Knipp, M. (1987) *Women, Western Education and Change: A Case Study of the Hausa-Fulani of Northern Nigeria*, DPhil dissertation, North Western University.

Mernissi, F. (1996) *Women's Rebellion and Islamic Memory*, Zed Books: London.

Thiam, A. (1991) *Speak Out, Black Sisters: Feminism and Oppression in Black Africa*, (translated by Dorothy S. Blair) Pluto Press: London.

Toynbee, P. (1997) 'In defence of Islamophobia', *The Independent*, 23 October 1997, p. 23.

About the author

Fatima L. Adamu is Professor in Sociology at Usmanu Dan Fodiyo University, Sokoto, Nigeria. She is Secretary of the women's health research network in Nigeria, Sokoto state, and has served on many government committees on family, women, and education.

Chapter 10

Islam and development: opportunities and constraints for Somali women

Sadia Ahmed

This chapter first appeared in *Gender & Development* Volume 7, Issue 1, March 1999, p. 69–72

Economic and social crisis can force communities to seek refuge in religious faith; in such situations, communities become more susceptible to the influence of groups which use religious beliefs as a means to gain power. Sadia Ahmed describes the effects on women's lives of the rise of Islamic extremism in Somalia since the early 1990s.

Introduction

In 1991, after 21 years of Siyad Barre's dictatorial regime, social and political upheavals brought Somalia to its knees: civil strife shredded the country into factions and the government finally collapsed, with disastrous consequences (for an account of the conflict, see Bradbury 1994). The conflict had a profound effect on the lives of the Somali people by destroying traditional economic systems, thus challenging women and men to change their respective economic roles.

Over the past two decades, extreme Islamic movements have gained momentum in Somalia (as elsewhere). I will examine some of the consequences for women of the rise of such groups, based on research carried out in 1996 by a coalition of grassroots women's organizations in Somalia's capital, Mogadishu.

Challenges to gender relations

Somalia's economy is mainly dependent on pastoralism. In the rural areas, livestock trade continues to be the backbone of the economy. Before the war, women from pastoralist groups were not usually directly involved in market transactions, and women's role in the economy seemed less significant than was actually the case. However, when it became difficult for men to travel for fear of government troops, the task of marketing livestock and buying foodstuffs and other goods for the family was increasingly – and continues to be – left to women (Warsame 1998). In urban areas, too, women's role in the economy became more visible. Today, although their incomes are generally low and the majority of female entrepreneurs have little or no education, women are increasingly forced to become the main breadwinner. The collapse of government has led to widespread unemployment among civil servants, and has forced more women into the marketplace, pressurized to meet their families' needs. The government was the main employer in Somalia; the voluntary and private sectors are relatively small.

The rise of religious extremism

The rise of religious extremist groups in Somalia began in the early 1970s, when the communist regime introduced the ideology of scientific socialism. A rebel movement promoting Islamic values arose; this was generally welcomed by people, who saw it as shoring up 'Somali' religious values and culture, and who felt a deep antipathy towards communism. Government crack-downs on this movement created further sympathy among the public, but over the years, support for Islamic groups has waned. Judging from my own conversations with Somalis, these groups are commonly perceived to be foreign-funded and -programmed. People also think that their agendas are incompatible with the interests of the Somali state. Extremists' mistakes, such as openly showing disrespect towards well-respected religious institutions, have led to further disillusionment on the part of the public. It has not proved easy to impose an extremist agenda on people who have been practising Muslims for centuries.

However, extreme Islamists do retain much support among certain social groups. Over the past decade in particular, they have found a large number of young male and female supporters who have grown up with little experience of life beyond conflict, with high unemployment rates and a lack of alternatives due to the destruction of schools. It is a well-known fact among Somalis that some extremist religious groups create business and employment opportunities for loyal followers (personal communication, 1998).

The impact of Islamic extremism on Somali women

Hasan (1991) lists the central Islamic principles which have been compromised by extremist groups in their quest for popularity and power, and suggests that the issue of women's roles and women's rights is the only one on which such groups will not compromise: 'for them, women's liberation movements (or associations) are the central enemy, because the entire patriarchal society, whose existence fundamentalism has gone to the defence of, is built upon the oppression of women' (Hasan 1991: 35).

Throughout the conflict and afterwards, Somali women's organizations in different parts of the country have been active in both development work and advocacy for peace. Currently, women's groups are challenging both the government and NGOs to recognize and promote the role of women in society, and to resist threats to their rights. Challenges have been made by religious extremists to women's rights within marriage and the family, to their economic and political participation outside the home, and to their freedom of dress and behaviour.

In 1996, a coalition of women's grassroots organizations in Mogadishu conducted a study on Somali women's rights from the perspective of Islam. The study was motivated by a concern about the increasing number of fundamentalist movements mushrooming throughout the country, and the implications of this for women and development; about a perceived low awareness among Somali women on women's rights in Islam; and about the tendency of groups of educated men to retain information or blatantly mislead women about their rights and duties.

The study was conducted using questionnaires of mainly closed-ended questions, designed to explore the level of respondents' awareness regarding women's rights. 120 people (80 women and 40 men from local communities) were interviewed. The findings confirmed that many women are confused about their rights, obligations, and duties as articulated in Islam. They also highlighted the fact that wholesome and unwholesome traditional practices tend to be associated with Islam, and with women's rights as defined in Islam. It reconfirmed that violations against Somali women's rights are culturally rooted, and that such practices continue unchecked (Sheck et al. 1996).

Marriage and the family

The widespread practice of relatively late marriage in Somalia is under threat. The national planning statistics of 1988 recorded the average age of marriage as 21 for girls, and 25 for boys; as more young people sought university education, the age of marriage was further postponed. However, this trend has been reversed by the collapse of the educational system. As fundamentalism strengthens its hold on the community, boys and girls are encouraged to marry ever earlier.

The Islamic principle of male responsibility for the family's maintenance, as outlined in the Qur'an (Afshar 1998), is being seriously undermined by young men being encouraged to marry one or more wives without economic means. The research confirmed that many young girls are ultimately either deserted or divorced. Since young couples sometimes marry without the parents' consent, deserted or divorced wives cannot always count on the support they could have otherwise relied on within the extended family system.

The research also suggests that ignorance of what the Qur'an says regarding polygamy is creating a problem for women. In 1998, I personally heard of a young girl under 20 with three children and little means, who was informed that her husband had married another woman; she calmly listened and defended him, saying 'it is his right' (personal communication, Sept 1998). In fact, the Qur'an sets out men's responsibility in single or polygamous marriages: polygamy is only permissible under strict social circumstances; it is therefore a conditional permission and not an article of faith or mortal necessity (Sheck et al. 1996).

Another development issue affecting women in their role within the family is fertility and family-planning. Spacing children is not a subject entertained by fundamentalists, despite the fact that the Qur'an encourages it; Islam gives women a wide range of rights, and does not oppose family-planning, especially when women's health is at stake. Early and frequent child-bearing increases young women's health risks.

Political and economic participation

Since the end of the war, Somalia has seen a decline of women's power in formal politics. The new political structures are principally based on clan relationships; it is becoming increasingly evident that unless parties free from clan politics are established, and the present strategy of fostering clan representation, common all over Somalia, is revisited, women's participation in politics will continue to be severely hampered. In Somaliland, as in Somalia, groups in power are using religion as the basis for excluding women from politics. A colleague who chairs the Umbrella Women's Organization in Hargeisa, Somaliland, recounted to me that every time they organized a workshop, the Minister of Justice and Religious Affairs came to interrogate participants about their activities, until he was officially asked by Parliament to stop this. He stated that his actions were based on his belief that women can be easily influenced by foreigners, and hence felt they needed protection (personal communication, 1998).

Veiling and control of behaviour

In Somalia, a society at war with itself, and where sexual violation has also become a tool of war, the tendency towards more extreme religious practice has been reinforced by the perceived need for protection and protective clothing. The number of veiled women in Somalia has visibly increased since 1991. Somali women's traditional dress is modest, but allows them freedom of movement and is thus more practical than the veil. As a Somali woman, I have seen that the recent increase in veiling has been accompanied, for the first time in Somali history, with extreme forms of censorship of women's behaviour, as extreme versions of Islamic interpretation have found fertile ground. Women who refuse to conform are harassed by both sexes, and peer pressure is exerted on them to veil.

Religious education and women's rights

Lack of religious education among the public allows extremists to use Islamic texts against women. Hadiths[1] are among the strongest weapons used to justify the marginalization of Muslim women from religious and social power. Although a significant portion of the accounts of the Prophet's comments and deeds were recounted on the authority of women (Ahmed 1990), the Hadiths were written by men. Many Hadiths that undermine women's freedom actually contradict the actions and philosophy of the Prophet Mohammed; the misogyny employed in the collection of such Hadiths has been discussed elsewhere (Mernissi 1991; Ahmed 1990). In addition, the fact that Arabic is not widely spoken in Somalia helps religious extremists to maintain their hold over communities: for example, they justify ideas about the weakness of women by arguing that the Arabic word *al nisaa* (the female) is synonymous with the Arabic word *nisf* (half). Through such arguments, women and men are made to believe that women are less intelligent in the eyes of Allah, and that the limitation of their rights is therefore justified. Until Somali women receive a better education, and better religious education in particular, this situation looks set to continue. Women's organizations are the only part of civil society to attempt seriously to redress the extremists' strategy of marginalizing women on the grounds of religious 'evidence'.

While the challenge of research and work by women's organizations is significant enough to cause concern to religious extremists and their supporters, their work is hindered by the lack of a coherent shared policy, and lack of access to the growing literature by Islamic scholars of both sexes, which challenges the denial of women's rights using religious texts. Women's organizations must bring about coherence in policy and achieve improved cooperation in designing and implementing strategies to challenge the erosion of women's rights.

Note

1   Reported accounts of the life of the Prophet Mohammed.

References

Ahmed, L. (1991) 'Women and the Advent of Islam' in *Women Living under Muslim Law*, Dossier 7/8, France.

Al Bushra, J. and Piza-Lopez, E. (1994) 'Gender, War and Food' in Macrae, J. and Zwi, A., Duffield, M.R. and Slim, H. (eds) *War and Hunger: Rethinking International Responses to Complex Emergencies*, SCF and Zed Books: London.

Baden, S. (1992) *The Position of Women in Islam Countries: Possibilities, Constraints and Strategies for Change*, report prepared for special programme, WID, Netherlands Ministry of Foreign Affairs (DGIS), Bridge.

Bradbury, M. (1994) *The Somali Conflict: Prospects for Peace*, Oxfam GB: Oxford.

Hasan, M. (1991) 'On Fundamentalism on our Land' in *Women Living under Muslim Law*, Dossier 11/12/13.

Mernissi, F. (1991) *The Veil and the Male Elite: A Feminist Interpretation of Women's Rights in Islam*, Addison-Wesley: UK.

Ragab, N. (1997) *The Record Set Straight: Women in Islam Have Rights*, an internet report, Islam (Submission to God) Web page, Musjid Tuscon, United Submitters International, USA. http://www.submission.org/hom. htm #WOM, Musjid Tuscon, USA, 1998.

Sheck, M., Ibrahim, H., Abdi, A. and Mohamed, F. (1996) *Report on Somali Women's Rights from the Perspective of Islam*, NOVIB report, Mogadishu.

Warsame, A. (1998) *The Civil War in Somalia: Differential Impact on Women and Men*, paper presented at a workshop on Resource Competition in Eastern Africa organized by the Institute of Social Studies (ISS) and OSSREA, 12–13 August 1998.

About the author

Sadia Ahmed was formerly the Director of the Women's Research Unit at the Somali Academy of Sciences and Arts, Somalia, and now works as gender co-ordinator for the Pastoral and Environmental Network in the Horn of Africa (PENHA).

Chapter 11

Abortion law reform in Latin America: lessons for advocacy

Gillian Kane

This chapter first appeared in *Gender & Development* Volume 16, Issue 2, July 2008, p. 361–75

Latin America's transition to democracy in the 1970s and 1980s was accompanied by the increased political participation of women, who demanded not only equal rights, but also insisted that addressing women's specific interests was key to establishing a truly representative democracy. Many in the Latin American women's movement saw the right to safe, legal abortion as fundamental. To date, their demand for this has gone largely unfulfilled, except in Cuba. There is no panacea to rescinding punitive abortion laws. However, the region is currently witnessing shifts in government policies on abortion, both progressive and retrogressive, which suggest that there is potential for substantive reform.

This chapter will use the recent experiences of Colombia, Mexico City, and Nicaragua to highlight shared challenges, establish linkages with other countries in the region, and demonstrate that the many different strategies which have been adopted present an opportunity to expand access to safe, legal abortion throughout Latin America.

Introduction: abortion in Latin America

According to the World Health Organization (WHO), 3.7 million unsafe abortions take place each year in Latin America and the Caribbean (Ahman and Shah 2004). Of these, approximately 2,000 result in death, accounting for 11 per cent of all maternal deaths (ibid.). With the exception of Cuba and Guyana, Latin America's abortion laws are extremely restrictive. In most nations, abortion is available for limited exceptions such as to save a woman's life, preserve her health, or for incest and rape. Others, like Nicaragua, Chile, and El Salvador prohibit abortion under any circumstances.

The adverse impact of the restrictions on abortion on the health of Latin American women is well-documented. A 2007 study published by the Guttmacher Institute and WHO, 'Induced Abortion: estimated rates and trends worldwide', found that strict prohibitions do not prevent abortions, but rather force women to terminate their pregnancies under unsafe conditions, often resulting in severe physical injuries or death (Sedgh et al. 2007). The penalization of abortion disproportionately affects poor and young women. Unlike middle- and upper-class women who can discreetly get a safe abortion at a private clinic, poor women must rely on suspect providers or self-administered abortions using traditional medicines and unsafe methods, which result in grave health consequences.

This chapter examines several recent changes in abortion policy in three different locations in Latin America, and examines the reasons behind the changes. In particular, it tries to draw out lessons for activists and advocates working on this and other similarly politically sensitive issues. Latin America has a strong tradition of abortion activism, and over the past three decades advocates have organized various initiatives aiming to ensure that where it is already legal, abortion is actually provided; and to legalize abortion and rescind punitive laws criminalizing the procedure, where these actions are required.

The successes of national and regional movements for abortion reform in Latin America can be measured primarily in terms of progressive changes in national legislation; increased capacity on the part of the movements and individual member organizations to advocate on the issues; and increased public consciousness of the issue. These successes are unique to Latin America. They have enabled the movement to advance, despite unfavorable political, legal, and social environments.

On 24 April 2007, Mexico City's legislative assembly passed one of the most comprehensive abortion reform bills in Latin America. The bill decriminalized abortion during the first 12 weeks of pregnancy, and required the Ministry of Health to fund all requests for the procedure. In Latin America, activists considered the event a watershed moment for Mexico, and for the region as a whole – the culmination of over 30 years of advocacy. Activism has also resulted in another recent legal change in Colombia, and other regional shifts in abortion policy – which are part of a broader transformation of the Latin American political landscape. In contrast, a recent setback in Nicaragua, where abortion for any reason has now been made a criminal offence, presents a cautionary tale.

This chapter draws on my experience working in the field of sexual and reproductive rights, with a specific focus on Latin America. I have extensive experience conducting research on secular and religious movements opposed to sexual and reproductive rights, and this work informs much of my analysis of the Catholic Church and evangelical Protestant movements referenced in this chapter. Currently, I serve as Assistant Program Officer for Latin America at the International Women's Health Coalition (IWHC). IWHC's Latin America Program provides sustained financial and professional support to our partners working in the region. Part of my work includes travel in the region where I meet with colleagues to support their efforts and strategize on approaches to advancing abortion rights in Latin America. Several IWHC partners are mentioned in this chapter.

The role of women's movements

Latin America's transition from dictatorships to democracy in the 1970s and 1980s was marked by the rise of a dynamic women's rights movement. Women's groups like the Mothers and Grandmothers of the Plaza de Mayo in Argentina, the *caceroleos* in Chile, trade unions in Uruguay, and the Casas de la Mujer (Women's Houses) in Nicaragua, were key to resisting military oppression (Kampwirth 2006). Yet, by joining with men in the collective struggle to overcome authoritarian regimes, women effectively subordinated their specific interests to the greater common goal of national liberation (Molyneux 1985). Even when socialist movements for reform, such as the Sandinistas in Nicaragua, did include commitments to address the 'gender interests' of women, these promises often went unfulfilled (ibid.).

By the 1990s, many in Latin America's women's movements were demanding equal rights, and insisted that addressing women's interests was fundamental to establishing a truly representative democracy. They called for the liberalization of laws regulating the human rights of individuals, which include not only the right to control one's body, but also the right to divorce,[1] the right to sexual orientation, and the decriminalization of abortion. Particular attention to women's reproductive rights has, in part, been spurred by the pioneering United Nations agreements of Cairo (1994) and Beijing (1995), which recognized for the first time that unsafe abortion was a major public-health concern, and that where legal, it should be safe and available to the full extent of the law: (Programme of Action, International Conference on Population and Development, 1994 Paragraph 8.20 (a); Programme of Action, Fourth World Conference on Women: Paragraph 106 (j)).

Across Latin America, women's organizing at the regional and national levels for abortion reform gained momentum in the wake of the conferences. The September 28th Campaign for the Decriminalisation of Abortion is a regional advocacy network, formed a few years before the UN conferences, in 1990. The campaign aimed to promote the liberalization of abortion laws, to counter conservative opposition to abortion, and to improve post-abortion services. By producing and distributing educational materials and newsletters, it facilitated a regional exchange of ideas and information, effectively assuring that abortion was continually in the minds of the public. Other organizations, for example the Latin American and Caribbean Committee for the Defense of Women's Rights (CLADEM), focused more generally on women's rights, and included advocacy on abortion as a significant part of their work.

Abortion and Church–state relations in Latin America

The abortion rights movement in Latin America has been impeded by strong opposition from the Catholic Church, which has close, historic ties to Latin American governments, and is the most influential religious and social tradition in the region.[2] The Catholic Church is immutable on certain issues, and remains unequivocally opposed to abortion, contraception, and divorce. Though there are notable exceptions where progressive movements within the Catholic Church, such as the liberation theology movement, are in fact conduits for change, these movements have not emphasized sexual and reproductive rights.

In recent years, the Catholic Church has found common ground on abortion with an unlikely ally: evangelical Protestant Christians. A steady increase in Catholic conversions to Protestantism is threatening the Church's religious hegemony in the region. Evangelical Protestants are also politically threatening, forming political parties and electing officials to prominent government positions throughout the region (Guatemala, for example, has had three evangelical presidents). Yet competition for new adherents has not prevented the rival churches from pulling together to advance the shared goal of criminalizing abortion (Llana 2006).

In the next sections, I examine recent changes to abortion policy in three different contexts: Nicaragua, Colombia, and Mexico City.

Recent changes to abortion policy

Nicaragua

In Nicaragua, abortion became a criminal offence in all circumstances in 2006. The partnership between the Catholic Church and evangelical Protestants was conspicuously on display in 2006 in Nicaragua, when Catholic Church leaders invited evangelical Protestants to join a massive rally in support of legislation outlawing abortion for any reason.[3] Although the Nicaraguan women's movements mobilized strongly, and were supported by many in the international reproductive rights and human rights community, the power of the religious bloc was too formidable. On 26 October 2006, Nicaragua's parliament voted 52:0 to criminalize therapeutic abortion, effectively denying Nicaraguan women access to abortion under any conditions.

Even before this, Nicaragua had one of the most restrictive laws in the region, allowing the procedure only for 'therapeutic' abortion.[4] Under Nicaragua's 1893 penal code, therapeutic abortion had no criminal penalty.[5] Nonetheless, access to legal abortion prior to the outlawing of therapeutic abortion was practically non-existent; in 2005, the Nicaraguan Ministry of Health reported providing only six therapeutic abortions (Pan-American Health Organization, citing Nicaragua Health Ministry in Aguilar 2007). It is important to note that, though few therapeutic abortions were actually provided when the procedure was legal, permitting abortion for that exception facilitated provision of corollary emergency obstetric care and treatments in the public-health system, many of them lifesaving.[6] Under the new therapeutic abortion ban, evidence is emerging that health-care providers are unwilling to perform emergency obstetric procedures – such as treatment for an ectopic pregnancy or postmenopausal hemorrhaging – fearing that these may be construed as an abortion, and subjected to criminal penalties.[7]

What precipitated the sudden urgency to change a century-old penal code? During the 2006 presidential elections – a tight race between the three presidential front-runners – the Catholic Church, supported by evangelical pastors, introduced legislation to repeal the country's law permitting therapeutic abortion.

The legislation was supported by parliamentarians from the two dominant parties, the right-wing Constitutionalist Liberal Party (PLC) and the Sandinista National Liberation Front (FSLN), both of which were vying for seats in the election and stood to gain needed support by currying favour with the Catholic Church. Several parliamentarians of both parties responded immediately by fast-tracking the Church's proposed legislation through parliament, a device primarily reserved for national emergencies (Blandon 2008). Their disregard for legislative protocol demonstrated the severe politicization of the abortion debate. Whereas the feminist movement in Nicaragua framed abortion reform as an issue of health, democracy, and individual rights – specifically, control over one's body and sexuality (Kampwirth 2006) – the Church effectively shifted the discourse to an explicitly religious agenda in the context of electoral politics.

Immediate opposition to the proposed ban came from the women's movement, which mobilized support from regional allies, as well as international organizations, including the United Nations and the European Union. Despite appeals from these organizations, from Nicaragua's Minister of Health, and from the medical community, to postpone the vote until after the elections- when debate would be unencumbered by electoral considerations – the legislation was presented and unanimously passed by the National Assembly, ten days prior to the elections. Incumbent President Enrique Bolaños immediately signed the legislation into law.

While Bolaños' action was disappointing to opponents of the ban, it was not surprising. What was shocking was the complete change of heart of former Sandinista president, Daniel Ortega, who had openly supported abortion during his tenure as president of Nicaragua in the 1980s. Ortega was one of three front-runners in the 2006 race; he made a show of his Catholic credentials, openly reconciled with the Catholic Church, and asserted that he was unequivocally against abortion. This move enabled him to campaign without incurring any criticism from the Catholic Church (Blandon 2008). A few days after the vote on abortion, on 6 November 2006, Ortega won by a comfortable 10 per cent majority.

Women's and human rights organizations have filed a petition with the Supreme Court of Nicaragua to declare the new law unconstitutional. Their claim contends that Nicaragua is violating international law – which prohibits bans on abortion – thereby denying women access to their basic rights to life and health. The Court has yet to respond, and the National Assembly ratified the abortion ban in September 2007. Today, any abortion performed in Nicaragua carries a criminal penalty of one to two years for the woman, or one to three years for the provider.

Events in Nicaragua have two main lessons for advocates. First, they demonstrate the need for constant vigilance throughout the region, to protect even the most limited access to abortion. Second, they show that politicians' support for abortion cannot necessarily be counted on, if the issue involves political risk. Ortega supported abortion during his first presidency when this posed no political risk, and quickly abandoned that position – and his wider support for the women's movement, which had been so important to the triumph of the Sandinistas in the 1980s[8] – when it became clear that doing so was politically expedient.

Colombia

In contrast, in May 2006, Colombia went from a total ban on abortion, to allowing it in cases of rape, malformation of the foetus, or danger to a woman's life or health.

Whereas change in Nicaragua was spurred by the actions of the Catholic Church, in a context of electoral politics, the Colombian modifications resulted from a two-year campaign which challenged the constitutionality of the law, using international human rights arguments. The campaign was led by Colombian attorney Monica Roa and built on three decades of work by the women's movement, which was supported at times by progressive parliamentarians.

Previous actions by activists in the women's movement were often defensive, in response to initiatives by the political Right and the Catholic Church to, for example, increase the penalties for abortion. These right-wing initiatives, like those in Nicaragua, shifted the discourse from health, gender, and rights to religious considerations,[9] and benefited from the unwillingness of parliamentarians to advance progressive legislation. Legal arguments supporting the criminalization of abortion were often framed within the context of the rights of the unborn, setting aside discussions of the rights of women to elect an abortion, or not to be obligated to carry a pregnancy forced on her through rape to term. Some legal arguments even included startling moral judgments, which concluded, for example, that 'a woman's dignity is not affected by the continuation of a pregnancy resulting from rape' (Posada 1997).

In 2005, Monica Roa, working with the international organization Women's Link Worldwide, judged that legal precedent, international law, and societal attitudes towards abortion had created an opening for rescinding Colombia's comprehensive abortion ban (Women's Human Rights Net 2005). She also judged that the country's Constitutional Court presented the most viable vehicle for reform, for several reasons. First, Colombia's Constitutional Court had recognized the legal significance of international human rights arguments and had used them to resolve constitutional challenges in other areas (Women's Human Rights Net 2005). Moreover, several international human rights arguments and agreements emerging in the past few decades, such as the Convention on the Elimination of All Forms of Discrimination Against Women (CEDAW), expressly advocated for liberalizing abortion for specific cases, contending that criminalizing abortion was in clear violation of women's rights (Roa 2006: 229).

Second, recent changes in the composition of the Constitutional Court – which included not only the first female judge, but also progressive judges who had included arguments against penalizing abortion in some of their judicial statements – indicated an openness to considering the issue of abortion. Finally, national surveys suggested that a majority of Colombians supported decriminalizing abortion for certain reasons.[10]

In April 2005, Monica Roa duly petitioned the Constitutional Court for review of Article 122 of the Colombian penal code, which criminalized all abortions under the country's penal codes. She argued that by denying women access to abortion, specifically in cases of rape, malformation of the foetus, or danger to a woman's life or health, the state of Colombia was not only violating women's right to equality, life, health, dignity, and reproductive autonomy, but was also violating its obligations under international treaties to protect women's right to life and health.[11]

In addition to her legal work, Roa developed a sophisticated communications strategy intended to 'change the way abortion was being debated', moving away from moral and religious discussions to considerations of gender equality, public health, and social justice (Batchelder 2008). The communications strategy took the 'extreme' position of the abortion rights movement's goal of total liberalization of abortion laws, and positioned it as a counterpoint to Roa's more modest demands, demonstrating that overturning the ban was a first step toward broader liberalization.[12]

The Catholic Church and its conservative allies mounted a vigorous counter-campaign, including personal attacks against Monica Roa. Nonetheless, in May 2006, the Court issued its landmark ruling that to make abortion a criminal act violated women's constitutional rights.

Women's Link Worldwide, and Monica Roa, are working to ensure that the Constitutional Court's decision is implemented, and that legal abortion services are available to women seeking them. Roa sees her work at the Constitutional Court as part of a larger strategy to generate change at the regional and international level (Roa 2006).

Roa's litigation at the Constitutional Court succeeded because of a favourable legal and social climate and her work with Women's Link Worldwide to promote women's rights through the implementation of international human rights law. Roa has made clear that her legal work was in many ways facilitated by, and built on, the advocacy work of the Colombian women's movement, which had for decades mobilized for the legalization of abortion.

Mexico City

The 2007 Mexico City decision to legalize abortion on demand within the first 12 weeks of pregnancy was the culmination of three decades of abortion advocacy by Mexico's women's and feminist movements.[13] The modern abortion movement was kick-started in 1976, when members of the National Movement for Women launched the initiative for Free and Legal Abortion and organized the First National Conference on Abortion (Brito 2007). Other initiatives to liberalize the country's penal codes regarding abortion followed – some even supported by incumbent presidents. However, these were stymied by the formidable opposition of the hierarchy of the Catholic Church and the conservative National Action Party (PAN), which is closely allied to the Church.[14]

By the 1990s, the movement for abortion reform gained momentum, garnering support not only from the women's and feminist movements, but also from various different sectors of Mexico's civil society, including prominent figures in the sciences and arts, such as Nobel-prize winner Octavio Paz Barraza.

With the 1999 election of Mexico City Mayor Rosario Robles, of the left-wing Democratic Revolutionary Party (PRD), the movement for abortion reform found a committed advocate who had political power and networks. In 2000, Robles' proposal to amend Mexico City's penal code to provide access for abortion after rape, and to lower the penalties for criminal abortion, was approved by Mexico City's Legislative Assembly. In a huge defeat for PAN and the Church, which appealed the decision to the Supreme Court of Justice, the constitutionality of the penal reforms was upheld in 2002, and the Secretary of Health quickly followed this by establishing norms regulating legal abortion in Mexico City, where almost a quarter of Mexico's total population lives.

In 2007, a collective of women's organizations drafted a bill which they presented to Mexico City's Legislative Assembly. The bill proposed decriminalizing all abortions up to 12 weeks of gestation; reducing the criminal sentences for abortions performed after 12 weeks; and modifying Mexico City's health laws to ensure free abortion services, education about sexual health and rights, and programmes to prevent unwanted pregnancies.[15] The bill was supported by different parts of society, including the science and medical community, and Mexico City's Mayor and Minister of Health. It was approved by the Legislative Assembly on 24 April 2007, by a 66:44 vote.

The Mexico City law is striking for its comprehensiveness; it not only makes abortion legal, but also requires the government to provide family-planning services to prevent unwanted pregnancies, and makes sexual and reproductive health care a government priority.

A confluence of social, legal, and political conditions in Mexico City enabled passage of the bill. First, public opinion favoured legalizing abortion; second, the women's movement and NGOs successfully positioned abortion as an issue of social justice and public health; third, trends in international discourse supported abortion as a human right of women; and fourth, the progressive composition of Mexico City's legislature ensured passage of the bill. As in Colombia, positioning abortion as a secular issue was a key advocacy strategy, particularly because preservation of the secular state is a paramount concern for most Mexicans.

At the time of writing (February 2008), two suits have been filed with the federal Supreme Court challenging the constitutionality of the law; it is anticipated that these will be voted on sometime in 2008. Advocates in Mexico are cautiously optimistic that the Supreme Court will support the decision to legalize abortion.

The road ahead

Over the past three decades, despite inhospitable political, legal, and social climates, regional activists have chipped away at legal barriers to abortion in Latin America. Sometimes, there have been setbacks. The Nicaragua example is more than this – for many, it is a catastrophe, which highlights the enormous challenges facing abortion rights advocates in the region. Yet in contrast, recent events in Colombia and Mexico City should hearten advocates for holistic approaches to women's health and rights, who see abortion as central to their vision. It is encouraging that the Mexico City decision demonstrates that it is possible, given the right political and social climate, to legalize all abortions in the first trimester, and also gain government commitment to pay for these services as well as provide educational programmes designed to prevent unwanted pregnancies. The case of Colombia, on the other hand, demonstrates that even in contexts where abortion has been outlawed completely, it is possible to make the case for allowing exceptions to protect the health and life of the woman, based on international law.

A key message which emerges from the case studies is that work on reform of laws regulating abortion must begin by reclaiming the terms of the debate from the Catholic Church, which has so successfully dominated the discourse by linking abortion to morality and religion. As the experiences of Mexico City and Colombia show, framing abortion within the context of reproductive health and rights, and using international law to support these arguments, is an effective tool in countering religious-based opposition.

Advancing work on this front could help by, if not circumventing, at least reducing, the possibility of future setbacks on abortion reform, as in Nicaragua. The case of Nicaragua also demonstrates that protecting even the most limited right to abortion is paramount.

Political will is certainly key in achieving progress on abortion, though it must be noted that leftist movements or parties are not *de facto* champions of the right to abortion. While the Democratic Party in the USA includes the right to abortion in its national platform, liberal parties and governments in Latin America do not. Avowed leftist presidents like Daniel Ortega in Nicaragua and Tabare Vazquez in Uruguay have publicly condemned abortion, citing Roman Catholic Church doctrine as the reason. Conversely, the conservative presidents of Mexico and Colombia, while not supporting abortion reforms in their countries, have also not impeded the legal process from going forward.

Lastly, the work of the women's movement in advocating for abortion reform is indispensable to progress on the issue. As all the above examples bear out, this vocal and active constituency is responsible for keeping the issue to the fore, and for assisting women to understand and access their rights.

Below, some of the key points which emerge from the case studies are highlighted, to conclude the chapter.

Legal policy reform

Abortion is categorized as a criminal act under most Latin American penal codes. As such, it is regulated under protocols adopted by executive bodies, which could potentially be changed through various legal means. An important insight is that activists need to identify the right point in the legal process at which to apply pressure for reform, and this varies in different countries. Activists in Mexico City, for example, worked with a legislative body, whereas Colombia petitioned for abortion reform through the superior court. In some contexts, legislative change can also be implemented through broader policy reform, that is, by proposing comprehensive health bills, which include the decriminalization of abortion, as has happened recently in Uruguay (Abracinskas 2007).

Building and working in coalitions

In addition to legal reform, coalition building is an important component of regional efforts to expand access to abortion. In the last decade, coalition building has benefited the abortion rights movement by enabling it to expand its base of support beyond the women's movement. As it works to strengthen the debate on abortion by shifting the discourse from 'women's interests' to the broader issue of heath, rights, and democracy, it is expanding its base of support. Activists are broadening alliances by engaging new partners from the medical, legal, and human rights communities. This was certainly the case in Mexico City where activists garnered support from a broad spectrum of the population, demonstrating a critical and diverse mass in support of reforming abortion.

Alliances with doctors and medical associations are particularly valuable for two reasons: as highly respected members of the community, they lend legitimacy and gravity to the movement, and, from a purely pragmatic perspective, without their support and willingness to perform abortions, access to abortion would be even more limited. Again, Mexico City provides a good example. By working to erode long-standing resistance from the medical community to support or perform abortions, the abortion rights movement was able to bring them into the coalition in support for reform, and engage them as vibrant activists, which certainly aided in passage of the bill. Indeed, their success was such that even Mexico's leading anti-abortion activist grudgingly conceded the medical community was no longer an ally because of their overt support for abortion (Tobar 2007).

Framing the issue appropriately for the context

Another companion to legal reform work is advocacy with governments and health ministries. Legal contexts and advocacy strategies vary between countries, but activists for abortion in Latin America as a region counter a common opposition: the Catholic Church supported by conservative political parties, and, increasingly, evangelical Protestants. To counter their cultural and moral influence, many abortion activists have begun promoting ideas about the separation of Church and state as a core part of their advocacy efforts.

Others, like Monica Roa in Colombia, have used international law as the legal framework for their work, refusing to engage directly in religious, or even medical, discussions on abortion. As discussed earlier, Roa's strategy was to emphasize that the state of Colombia was in violation of international law. Debating the merits or shortcomings of abortion based on the viability or the humanity of a foetus would have diluted her arguments and detracted from her case (Batchelder 2008).

Still others, like activists in Uruguay's feminist movements, are working to frame abortion within the context of public health (Abracinskas 2007). In 2004, the abortion rights movement presented the Uruguayan parliament with a comprehensive reproductive-health bill that would legalize abortion in the first trimester. The bill went through a series of fits and starts and now faces its final hurdles; in 2007 the Senate passed the bill and it now awaits a vote from the House of Representatives, where it is expected to pass. Leftist President Tabare Vasquez says he will veto the bill, and the abortion rights movement is working to refine its response strategy in anticipation of the veto (Abracinskas 2008).

Public education and awareness-raising

In addition to lobbying for legal reform to ensure that women eligible under existing law have access, advocates in Latin America are working to ensure that women are informed about the legality and availability of abortion and can access services. This has involved educational and outreach campaigns for women community leaders and youth, as well as intense media work to educate and sensitize populations about health and rights as they pertain to abortion. In Peru, where abortion is legal for the ambiguously termed 'therapeutic' reasons, organizations like the Center for the Promotion and Defense of Sexual and Reproductive Rights (PROMSEX) are working at the grassroots level to inform women and community leaders about specific exceptions covered under the category of therapeutic abortion (Guerrero 2007).

Capacity-building and technical assistance

Another important area of work is the provision of clear guidelines to ensure that the law is implemented, in countries where safe legal abortion is available. This requires knowledge and technical assistance, supplied to public-health systems and used in training health-care workers and providers. Where it is legal, abortion is supported by clear guidelines for implementation. Some NGOs, for example Catholics for the Right to Decide, of Brazil, are filling gaps by working to improve the quality of legal abortion services, and to increase the number of hospitals offering legal abortion (Neto and Rebouças 2002). WHO has written a technical guide to safe abortion, recommending strategies for designing effective programmes, and its materials support this work.

Notes

1   The legalization of divorce is a recent phenomenon in the region. For decades the Catholic Church hierarchy, arguing on the basis of the sanctity of marriage, had presented stiff opposition to advocates for legalizing divorce. Chile only legalized divorce in 2004, Argentina in 1987, and Brazil in 1977.

2   It should of course be noted that the Church's influence on, and engagement with, governments in Latin America pre-dates the military regimes of the last century (Htun 2003: 30). In the early 1960s the Vatican hosted the Second Vatican Council, which effectively modernized aspects of Church practices. It also emphasized women's relative equality to men and their importance within the Church. However, equality was always understood within the context of the family and home, and did not extend to support for women's individual rights. While there were some very modest improvements for women under military governments in Latin America – family law reforms and women's property rights – the authoritarian regimes wholeheartedly embraced the Church's traditional view of women as good mothers and wives and did not grant women additional individual rights (ibid.: 33).

3   Cardinal Miguel Obando y Bravo, the former cardinal of Managua, led the march of Catholics and evangelicals numbering in the tens of thousands to the National Assembly, two weeks before the elections.

4   Therapeutic abortion was not regulated under Nicaraguan law; rather it was guided by an official Health Ministry norm that permitted the procedure for risk to the life or health of the woman, or for malformation of the foetus.

5   A 2007 report on abortion in Nicaragua by Human Rights Watch concluded it was unlikely that anyone had been prosecuted for providing or receiving an abortion (Møllmann 2007).

6   Based on the 2007 Pan-American Health Organization (PAHO) report 'Derogation of Therapeutic Abortion in Nicaragua: Impact on Health', citing Nicaragua's Health Ministry (Aguilar 2007). Human Rights Watch noted that 'Nicaragua's Health Ministry estimates that formerly 10 percent of all pregnancies ended in an abortion or miscarriage, totalling approximately 7,500 abortions and miscarriages in 2005', and that 'the remaining abortions and miscarriages treated in the public health system in 2005 were: 397 ectopic pregnancies (not officially classified as abortion), 232 cases of molar pregnancies, 1183 other abnormal pregnancies, 211

miscarriages, 49 other abortions, and over 5,400 non-classified abortions, some of which might have originally been induced illegally' (Møllmann 2007).

7 Human Rights Watch has documented the deleterious consequences of the one year ban, including the denial of access to life- or health-saving services (Møllmann 2007).

8 The critical role of women in the Nicaraguan revolution is well documented; they constituted 30 per cent of the revolutionary forces, were politically active, and provided logistical and back-up support to combatants. See Molyneux 1985.

9 Indeed, a 1997 decision by Colombia's Constitutional Court went so far as to cite a papal encyclical to legally justify penalizing abortion (Roa 2006).

10 A 2003 survey of Colombian men and women who self-identified as Catholics demonstrated they condone abortion when: the woman's life is in danger (73 per cent), the woman's health is at risk (65 per cent), in cases of serious physical or mental foetal impairment (61 per cent), and/or the pregnancy is the result of rape (52 per cent) (Source: www.catholicsfor-choice.org/news/pr/2005/20050414colombiaabortion.asp (last accessed April 2008); Women's Human Rights Net 2005.)

11 The Center for Reproductive Rights successfully argued two cases of abortion based on international human rights law. 'In K.L. v. Peru, the United Nations Human Rights Committee found the Peruvian government at fault for its failure to ensure access to legal abortion services. The plaintiff in that case was a young woman who was forced by state employed health officials to carry a fatally impaired fetus to term. In a similar case in Mexico, brought before the Inter-American Commission on Human Rights, the Mexican government agreed to a settlement ensuring reparations for a 13-year-old rape victim who was denied access to a legal abortion' (2006). 'Landmark decision by Colombia's highest court liberalizes one of the world's most restrictive abortion laws', www.reproductiverights.org/pr_06_0511colombia.html (last accessed February 2008).

12 Roa also emphasized that in addition to the work of the Colombian women's movement, the international women's movement was fundamental in developing the international human rights standards that comprised the basis of her case (Women's Human Rights Net 2005).

13 Abortion is regulated under Mexico's penal code which criminalizes abortion, though all of the county's 32 states have provisions decriminalizing the procedure for rape, and many others also include exceptions for the health or life of the mother; malformation of the foetus; and even for economic reasons.

14 For more on the PAN and the Catholic Church see Gonzalez Ruiz 2001.

15 The bill not only reduced the sentences for abortions after 12 weeks from one to three years of imprisonment to three to six months or 100 days of community service, but it also stipulated that pregnancy begins at implantation, a critical definition which helps 'to determine gestational age as well as reinforce the legality of assisted reproduction, investigation in embryos and therapeutic cloning' (Barraza 2007).

References

Abracinskas, L. (2007) *Aborto en Debate: Dilemas y Desafíos Uruguay Democrático*, Montevideo: Mujer y Salud en Uruguay (MYSU).

Abracinskas, L. (2008), correspondence with author.

Aguilar, R. (ed) (2007), 'Derogation of therapeutic abortion in Nicaragua: Impact on health', Pan-American Health Organization (PAHO).

Ahman, E. and Shah, I. (2004) *Global and regional estimates of the incidence of unsafe abortion and associated mortality in 2000* 4th edn, World Health Organization: Geneva.

Barraza, E. (2007) *Miradas Sobre el Aborto*, Grupo de Información en Reproducción Elegida, Mexico.

Batchelder, E. (2008) 'An Interview with Monica Roa', *A: The Abortion Magazine* 3, IPAS: North Carolina.

Blandon, M.M. (2008) correspondence with author.

Brito, E. (2007) 'Los inicios de la lucha por aborto libre y gratuito', *Cimacnoticias* www.cimacnoticias.com/site/s07040308-OPINION-Los-inicio.17104.0. html (last accessed March 2008)

Center for Reproductive Rights (2006) 'Landmark decision by Colombia's highest court liberalizes one of the world's most restrictive abortion laws', www.reproductiverights.org/pr_06_0511colombia.html (last accessed January 2008)

Gonzalez Ruiz, E. (2001) *La Ultima Cruzada: De los Cristeros a Fox*, Grijalbo: Mexico City.

Guerrero, R. (2007) 'Lo que debes saber sobre tu derecho al aborto terapeutico' Lima : PROMSEX.

Htun, M. (2003) *Sex and the State: Abortion, Divorce, and the Family under Latin American Dictatorships and Democracies*, Cambridge: Cambridge University Press.

Kampwirth, K. (2006) 'Resisting the feminist threat: antifeminist politics in post-Sandinista Nicaragua', *NWSA Journal* 19(2): 77–90.

Llana, S. (2006) 'Evangelicals flex growing clout in Nicaragua's election', *Christian Science Monitor* November 2, 2006.

Møllmann, M. (2007) 'Over Their Dead Bodies: Denial of Access to Emergency Obstetric Care and Therapeutic Abortion in Nicaragua', *Human Rights Watch* 19(2b).

Molyneux, M. (1985) 'Mobilization without emancipation? Women's interests, the state, and revolution in Nicaragua', *Feminist Studies* 11(2): 229–41.

Neto, J.A. and Rebouças, R.A. (2002) *Aborto Legal: Compartilhando Experiencias*, Católicas pelo Direito a Decidir.

Posada, C. (1997) 'Abortion: a social, legal and juridical debate of the first order in Colombia', *Reproductive Health Matters* 9: 147–8.

Roa, M. (2006) 'El Proyecto LAICIA (Litigio de Alto Impacto en Colombia: la Inconstitucionalidad del Aborto)', in Checa, S. (eds) *Realidades y Coyunturas del Aborto: Entre el Derecho y la Necesidad*, Buenos Aires: Paidos.

Sedgh, G., Henshaw, S., Singh, S., Ahman, E. and Shah, I. (2007) 'Induced abortion: estimated rates and trends worldwide', *The Lancet* 370: 1338–45.

Tobar, H. (2007) 'Abortion is out of the shadows in Mexico City', *Los Angeles Times*.

Women's Human Rights Net (2005) 'Challenging abortion law in Colombia: an interview with Monica Roa', Association for Women's Rights in Development, www.whrnet.org/docs/interview-roa-0507.html (last accessed March 2008)

World Health Organization (2003) 'Safe abortion: technical and policy guidance for health systems', Geneva: World Health Organization.

About the author

Gillian Kane is Senior Policy Advisor for IPAS. She previously worked as Assistant Programme Officer for Latin America at the International Women's Health Coalition (IWHC). IWHC's Latin America Programme provides sustained financial and professional support to partners working in the region.

Chapter 12

Conclusion: moving forward

Emma Tomalin

Reviewing the main themes

The chapters in this volume indicate that the relationships between religion, gender and development are complex and context dependent. They also emphasize the importance of considering religion as a relevant factor in gender and development research, policy and practice.

Development has tended to have an 'uneasy relationship' with religion (Ver Beek 2000). Until recently, considerations of religion and spirituality were largely absent from development policy, and development practitioners have made inadequate use of them to shape their decision-making processes about which organizations to partner with and support.

Over the past decade exploring the relationship between development and religion has become more common and popular. Academics have considered the relationships between religion and development, and their impacts on gender roles and relations. In parallel, partnerships between religion (in the forms of faith-based organizations and religious leaders) and development donors have grown. Many commentators have welcomed this shift, firstly because it acknowledges the global relevance of religion in understanding how people approach problems, and also because it recognizes the significant role that faith-based organizations and religious individuals play in the provision of welfare and development-related services (Clarke and Jennings 2007).

Where the promotion of gender justice conflicts with religious thought and practice, this has implications for many aspects of women's lives. Reproductive rights, sexuality, marriage, legal equality, violence, civil status, harmful traditional practices, or gender relations in general can become the focus for conflict. Moreover, the rise of religious extremisms and fundamentalisms within different faiths and in different places has exacerbated risks for women in ways that can be harmful to their physical and mental health.

At the same time, different expressions of 'religious feminism' are increasingly present within all religions. In some cases, these aim to tackle religiously-based gender inequality by providing alternative interpretations of religious texts and teachings. In highly religious contexts, and in places where the promotion of development and women's rights agendas may be perceived as 'Western interference', engagement with religious texts, leaders and organizations may support more appropriate and successful approaches to gender-aware development. Women may also find that being part of a religious tradition provides them with emotional and practical support, and many benefit from services provided by faith-based organizations. However, the extent to which religious feminisms are able to influence and negotiate change varies widely between contexts (Tadros 2010: 13–14).

Considerations of *how* development research, policy and practice engage with religion are just as important as arguments about the need for engagement. Although most of the writers in this volume consider that the inclusion of religion in development is potentially beneficial for women, others are concerned that the attention now placed on religion by Western governments and donors is promoting styles of religious identity, organizational forms and discourses that could have negative impacts on already delicate gender regimes. The interaction between efforts to improve the position of women on the one hand, and recognition of the importance of religion on the other, requires careful, critical analysis. Without this, there is a danger that bringing religion into development may undermine the progress that has been made to mainstream gender equity into development processes (Pearson and Tomalin 2007; Tadros 2010; 2011).

In this conclusion my aim is to consider the main themes raised in the introduction in relation to the challenges of the future. What challenges and opportunities are likely to be encountered by development research, policy and practice in negotiating the relationships between religion, gender and development? What tools and strategies can we employ to navigate this terrain? Where do we need to direct future research so that engagement between development and religion can result in positive outcomes for women and gender equality?

The 'rush to find the religious'

In a recent special issue of the IDS Bulletin, *Gender, Rights and Religion at the Crossroads*, Mariz Tadros argues that since 9/11 the international community has begun to promote a 'religious' approach in its dealings with Muslim communities (Tadros 2011: 1). Religion has become an entry point through which development policy makers and practitioners seek to gain a foothold in Muslim communities when approaching issues around women's rights. 'Applications from grantees wanting to make a good pitch for donor funding are increasingly incorporating the participation of clergymen in their funding proposals as partners and stakeholders' (*ibid.*: 3). However, as Cassandra Balchin warns, 'this rush to "find the religious" is rarely backed by sophisticated knowledge of the diversities among religious groups' (2011: 17). Hania Sholkamy also cautions that 'using religion as the pathway to gender justice is not a smooth strategy. It can work well but may cause stumbling when the pathway becomes more important than the destination' (2011: 49).

While the engagement between development and religion is most prominent with respect to Islam, these debates have gained broader relevance across diverse religious traditions. Development policy and practice should not become a slave to religious solutions, and not all development strategies need to refer to religion. It is essential to listen to women's voices, and to ensure that development responses are built on a sound understanding of the context. Although in some locations engaging with religious texts, religious leaders and faith-based organizations can be a useful strategy in promoting female education or reproductive health, it is important to assess potential allies carefully to ensure that they are committed to diversity and gender equality.

In addition to the interest in religion as a basis for addressing women's rights, donors show increasing interest in funding and supporting faith-based organizations that provide services to women. Mariz Tadros outlines three arguments that are sometimes employed in support of the role of faith-based organizations in providing such services:

1   Religious leaders and organizations play an influential role at the grassroots level. This can be capitalized upon to promote gender equality;
2   Religious organizations are the basis of social networks, which women draw on as part of their daily survival strategies; and
3   Some forms of assistance are indigenous and in tune with the grassroots realities of women, as well as representing an alternative form of development that responds to women's spiritual and material needs. (2010: 9)

The danger is that these 'arguments' turn into assumptions that guide development policy and practice rather than being part of a series of considerations that might or might not be appropriate, depending on the situation. Building on this idea, I explore some of the potential dilemmas that engaging with faith-based organizations and religious leaders pose for gender and development.

1 Finding out about, understanding and engaging with faith-based attitudes towards gender

It is often difficult to find out about a faith-based organization's attitudes towards gender issues. Development practitioners may be wary about openly critiquing religious organizations or leaders when their attitudes towards gender are problematic. Alternatively, some staff may be reluctant to engage with religion and religious organizations, either because they feel they lack sufficient knowledge to do so, or because they are concerned about being perceived to 'interfere in local culture' (Hopkins and Patel: 62).

This points to the need for gender and development practitioners to develop understanding and trust with faith communities and to engage in activities that are guided by detailed knowledge of the particular situation. It is also important to promote 'religious literacy' – knowledge of religion and religious organizations in the local context – as an important skill for development workers. In some situations, as the chapter in this volume on the work of Tearfund by Mandy Marshall and Nigel Taylor suggests, other faith-based organizations that share the same faith background may be better placed to delve into the gender attitudes of religious organizations and to suggest change where these attitudes are found to be problematic.

2 Women's agency in faith-based organizations and 'food-for-faith'

Considering the highly patriarchal nature of most religions, women's participation in religious institutions (e.g. churches, mosques) and faith-based organizations is likely to be marginal as they are so often excluded from positions of leadership and decision-making processes. Mariz Tadros suggests that even when women do have opportunities for leadership in faith-based organizations, this does not necessarily challenge traditional gender relations (2010).

While religion can provide women with coping strategies and concrete support services, this may also involve gender costs. For example, faith-based organizations may provide women with a range of spiritual and social services while at the same time limiting their freedoms. In some situations, women's access to welfare services provided by religious organizations may be conditional on them adopting religiously appropriate gender roles and behaviour. This suggests the need for careful evaluation before alliances are formed with faith-based organizations.

3 Do faith-based organizations and religious leaders represent women's interests?

The capacity of faith-based organizations and religious leaders to support women's 'spiritual development' as well as their 'material development', is sometimes cited as an advantage. In addition, faith-based organizations and religious leaders are often typified as being closer to the grassroots and therefore being in a position to reflect women's best interests.

Although some faith-based organizations are undoubtedly grounded in local communities, others 'seek to impose their own values and ideologies' instead of responding to locally expressed gender priorities (Tadros 2010: 11). We cannot simply assume that religious leaders understand the facts of women's lives and needs, or that they necessarily have gender equality as a goal.

Because faith-based organizations are not primarily motivated by gender concerns, their engagement with gender issues may seem contradictory. Some of their actions may appear to support gender equity while others undermine it. For example, in Malawi, Muslim, Catholic and Protestant faith-based organizations opposed harmful widowhood practices. Yet the same organizations simultaneously opposed a government campaign promoting condom use (Tadros 2010: 11). Engagement with faith-based organizations needs to be underpinned by an understanding of their gender politics, and of the broader social, political and economic context in which they operate.

In the remainder of this chapter, I will discuss three areas of recent academic research that raise important conceptual and practical issues for future work on religion, gender and development.

The implications of religion for development: a means to an end or a basis for dialogue?

Some commentators criticize development organizations and donors for merely wanting to use religion instrumentally, to achieve their ends, rather than recognizing that it might challenge their goals and conception of development more deeply. Séverine Deneulin and Masooda Bano argue that development donors engage with religion on particular issues that suit 'what [they] conceive of as valuable and desirable development outcomes' (2009: 25).

For members of religious traditions, the values and long-term goals of belonging to that tradition may well conflict with or challenge some aspects of development priorities. For example, such critics may consider that the mainstream development agenda ignores the 'spiritual' aspects of people's lives in pursuit of the material and that the ethical foundations of their religion is at odds with the dominant capitalist underpinnings of development. Some members of religious traditions may also argue that gender difference is fixed according to divine sanction, but that this does not mean that women should be oppressed or subject to violence because of it.

Should the inclusion of religion force us to theorize or practise development differently? What trade-offs, compromises or tensions does this entail for the pursuit of gender equality?

For instance, when we engage with religious actors around gender concerns we cannot assume that all parties subscribe to a unified feminist vision. The success and ambitions of religious feminisms in different contexts are likely to be highly variable. Nonetheless, in many contexts there is a genuine commitment to exploring women's empowerment within a religious framework, even if by Western feminist standards the goals might sometimes seem quite modest.

Séverine Deneulin and Masooda Bano argue that in many Muslim countries, development initiatives around women's rights have tended to support interventions that are influenced by Western feminist thinking. In engaging with a Westernized elite they have marginalized 'Muslim women, in particular the Islamic female leadership' (2009: 25). They contrast different notions of women's empowerment held by secular women's rights NGOs and female madrasas in Pakistan. Whereas the secular organizations stress 'individual liberty, including sexual liberty, and participation of women in economic and political affairs' (2009: 160) the madrasas have focused on women's interests being 'best served in a stable family unit ... [where] the emphasis is not on equality but on equity' (ibid.). They suggest that through 'dialogue', where each group attempts to understand the other point of view, combined activism to improve gender relations is likely to be more successful than a situation where each side is unwilling to compromise and pursues separate agendas.

Such examples show us how religious feminisms may not map exactly onto gender and development goals, but can enable women to improve their lives through negotiating religious boundaries in culturally appropriate ways. This approach requires a clearer understanding of what constitutes women's empowerment in different contexts, and openness to including a diversity of views and approaches even when they clash with secular feminisms based on the pursuit of female and male equality in all spheres of life. Research that addresses this could assist development actors in modifying their language and expectations in different contexts so as to support approaches to female empowerment that are culturally embedded and appropriate, and therefore achieve the best outcomes for women at any particular time. Research that addresses the tensions as well as the instances of successful interaction between secular and religious actors around gender concerns can be useful in highlighting areas where they are likely to agree as well as potential flashpoints to be negotiated or even avoided.

Rethinking the boundaries between the religious and the secular

Development discourses have sometimes assumed that moves towards secularism are inherently positive for women's rights, since the influence of religion will be reduced within politics and the public sphere. Recent research shows that this is too simplistic. Shahra Razavi and Anne Jenichen argue for the need to revisit discussions about secularism and theories of secularization and the implications of these for women's rights (2010).

Secularization is sometimes understood as meaning that religion will become a purely private matter, playing less of a role in public life over time. Some researchers argue that in fact the opposite is true, and that religion is being 'de-privatised' and becoming increasingly present in the public sphere (Casanova 1994). Others maintain that religion has never been a purely private affair and has always had an impact upon various aspects of social and political life, even in contexts where there is a constitutional separation between religion and the state (Razavi and Jenichen 2010: 835).

In addition, an understanding of secularism as state non-interference in religious matters may actually allow inequality in family and personal customs to continue outside the domain of state law (for example in 'personal law' in India). The notion that religion in the private sphere is freely chosen and directed towards one's relationship with the divine – or towards making one feel better in difficult times – may have some validity, but ignores the broader impacts of religion on women's lives where it can act as a tool of control and oppression in the private domain.

The assumption that secularism is good for women overlooks the ways in which the private is political and the family is 'public', in the sense of exerting an external influence on women that is often beyond their control. We need a more mature and realistic account of secularism and secularization which pays attention to the actual way that religion operates in women's lives at both the public and the private levels, and which is accompanied by the space for appropriate responses to develop.

Oppositions between public and private, secular and religious, are inadequate as frameworks to accommodate the diverse ways that religion influences women's oppression as well as the opportunities that engaging with religion can offer for women's empowerment and development. For example, one of the key messages of this book is that the line between different feminisms, secular and religious, is more blurred than we once thought. As Shahra Razavi and Anne Jenichen write: 'it is also unhelpful to set up an opposition between internally and externally generated change, or to represent one avenue as superior to the other. The dividing line between the two may also be porous, as those who work for 'internal reform' very often draw on the ideas and arguments of 'external' advocates for change. Alliances between feminists of different religious and secular communities are therefore imperative' (2010: 846).

Moreover, alongside the rise of various fundamentalist and extreme versions of religion, we also find a strengthening of transnational women's movements, constituted by networks of regional groups and movements that promote their own strategies for women's empowerment. Organizations such as Women Living Under Muslim Laws and Catholics for a Free Choice, as well as movements within religious traditions around issues such as female ordination, all suggest the growth of vibrant transnational feminist networks that aim to negotiate women's empowerment within local religious and cultural contexts. This contrasts with earlier styles of international feminism that were often perceived as Western-driven and top-down, favouring 'secular' approaches and values (Tomalin 2009; Moghadam 2000).

Women's social movements and development

Despite the growing presence of religious actors in women's movements for social change, this is an area that remains under-researched. This can partly be attributed to the fact that feminists and development practitioners often view religion as being a hindrance to the achievement of gender equality.

While women's movements globally have tended to take a secular route, many of the campaigns and issues that they address are linked to religion in important and complex ways. Increasingly, women's movements, particularly in developing countries, have had to face difficult questions with regards to their position on religion as it is both a potential barrier to, as well as a driver of, social change. The public influence of religion is arguably becoming more prominent across the globe, while at the same time there are concerns that 'fundamentalist' or 'extreme' versions of religion (that are typically conservative in their attitude towards women) are gaining a firmer foothold in civil society and within the state. In such a climate, there is a need for empirical studies and theoretical reflection that explore the ways that religion can act as a barrier as well as a positive force in the achievement of gender equality and women's rights.

For instance, recent research in Nigeria indicates that with respect to the campaign to reflect CEDAW in domestic law, religious opposition was successful in blocking legal change (Para-Mallam et al. 2011). Conversely, religious groups were instrumental in the success of a campaign to enact legislation to outlaw harmful widowhood practices (Adamu et al. 2011).

In both of these cases, the aim was to influence those in power to make legal changes in women's favour. Duncan Green argues that those who wish to design strategies to influence decision makers need to understand who are the 'champions, shifters, and blockers' of change; they need to consider with whom they might seek to form alliances and coalitions; and they need to be wary of 'pre-emptive reforms by the powerful' (Green 2008: 439–40).

Conclusion

My aim in this conclusion was to summarize the key points raised in the introduction to the book and to consider them in relation to the challenges of the future. In particular, I have identified a tension between the 'rush to find the religious' as a positive shift in development policy and practice, and the observation that in the absence of sustained and careful research, engagement with religious leaders and faith-based organizations runs the risk of exacerbating already fragile gender regimes. The emerging openness to thinking about and engaging with religion in development therefore offers both challenges and opportunities for working in gender and development. The chapters in this volume offer insights from empirical research as well as outlining evolving themes and good practice that will be of interest to students, researchers and development policy makers and practitioners.

References

Adamu, Fatima, Adebayo O. Ajala, Olufunmilayo J. Para-Mallam and Bolatito Lanre-Abass (2011) 'Engagements of Women's Movements with Religion in the Promotion of Women's Rights through Legal Reform in Anambra State, Nigeria', RaD Working Paper 60, University of Birmingham, Birmingham.

Balchin, Cassandra (2011) 'Religion and development: a practitioner's perspective on instrumentalisation', *IDS Bulletin* 42(1): 15–20.

Casanova, Jose (1994) *Public Religions in the Modern World*, University of Chicago Press, Chicago.

Clarke, Gerard and Mike Jennings (2007) *Development, Civil Society and Faith-Based Organizations*, Palgrave, Basingstoke.

Deneulin, Séverine and Masooda Bano (2009): *Religion in Development: Rewriting the Secular Script*, Zed Books, London.

Green, Duncan (2008) *From Poverty to Power: How Active Citizens and Effective States can Change the World*, Oxfam International, Oxford. Available from: http://www.oxfam.org.uk/resources/downloads/FP2P/FP2P_BK_Whole.pdf

Hopkins, Adrienne and Kirit Patel (2006) 'Reflecting on gender equality in Muslim contexts in Oxfam GB', *Gender & Development* 14(3): 434.

Moghadam, V. (2000) 'Transnational feminist networks: collective action in an era of globalization', *International Sociology* 15(1): 57–85.

Para-Mallam, Oluwafunmilayo J., Bolatito Lanre-Abass, Fatima Adamu, and Adebayo Ajala (2011) 'The Role of Religion in Women's Movements for Social Change: The Campaign for the Domestication of CEDAW in Nigeria', RaD Working Paper 59, University of Birmingham, Birmingham.

Pearson, Ruth and Emma Tomalin (2007) 'Intelligent design? A gender sensitive interrogation of religion and development', in G. Clarke and M. Jennings (eds), *Development, Civil Society and Faith-Based Organizations*, pp. 46–71, Palgrave, Basingstoke.

Razavi, Shahra and Anne Jenichen (2010): 'The unhappy marriage of religion and politics: problems and pitfalls for gender equality', *Third World Quarterly* 31(6): 833–50.

Sholkamy, Hania (2011) 'Creating conservatism or emancipating subjects? On the narrative of Islamic observance in Egypt', *IDS Bulletin* 42(1): 47–55.

Tadros, Mariz (2010) 'Faith-Based Organizations and Service Delivery Some Gender Conundrums', UNRISD Gender and Development Programme Paper Number 11. Available from: http://www.unrisd.org/unrisd/website/document.nsf/8b18431d756b708580256b6400399775/592137c50475f6a8c12577bd004fb5a0/$FILE/Tadros.pdf

Tadros, Mariz (2011) 'Introduction: gender, rights and religion at the crossroads', *IDS Bulletin* 42(1): 1–9.

Tomalin, Emma (2009) 'Buddhist feminist transnational networks, female ordination and women's empowerment', *Oxford Development Studies* 37(22): 81–100.

Ver Beek, Kurt (2000) 'Spirituality: a development taboo', *Development in Practice* 10(1): 31–43.

About the author

Emma Tomalin is Senior Lecturer, Department of Theology and Religious Studies, University of Leeds

Annotated bibliography

1 Special issues of journals

Third World Quarterly: **The Unhappy Marriage of Religion and Politics: Problems and Pitfalls for Gender Equality (2010 31:6).**

This publication draws upon working papers from an UNRISD research programme on 'Religion, Politics and Gender'.[1] It explores religion as a political force and the ways in which it influences the struggles for gender equality in different contexts. The articles are from a range of contexts and religious traditions, including Islam in Pakistan, India, Turkey, Iran and Nigeria; Judaism in Israel; Christianity in Nigeria, Serbia, Chile, Mexico, Poland and the USA; and Hinduism in India.

Journal of International Women's Studies: **Gender and Islam in Asia (2009 11:1).**

The articles in this special issue focus on gender and Islam in Asia in a bid to address a lack of publishing from and about this region when compared to the Middle East. Many of the articles are concerned with addressing the ways in which women work within an Islamic framework to pursue empowerment. It includes papers about Uzbekistan, Indonesia, Malaysia, India, the USA, Turkey, Afghanistan, Sri Lanka, Pakistan and Bangladesh.

Women's Studies International Forum: **From Village Religion to Global Networks: Women, Religious Nationalism and Sustainability in South and Southeast Asia (2010 33:4).**

The articles in this special issue come from an international workshop held in New Delhi in 2007. The workshop explored the influence of the increase of politicized religion on aspects of 'traditional' religious behaviour that can be seen as positive and supportive of human and environmental sustainability, as well as its impact for inter-religious and community relations as communal barriers intensify. There are eight papers on Bangladesh, three on India and Pakistan, and five from Southeast Asia.

IDS Bulletin: **Gender, Rights and Religion at the Crossroads (2011 42:1).**

This publication argues that this is a crucial moment for engaging with the politics of religion and gender. Since the events of 9/11 'Muslim communities' have emerged as political categories and this has specific implications for thinking about and addressing women's human rights. The articles deal with topics from a range of countries and regions, including Turkey, Afghanistan, India and Egypt as well as others that are cross-cultural.

2 Working papers found on the Religions and Development (RaD) research programme website *(www.rad.bham.ac.uk/)*

Funded by DFID between 2005 and 2010, and based at the University of Birmingham, the RaD website offers a range of literature reviews, background papers and working papers that explore the complex relationships between religions and international development. A number of the papers have a gender focus. Of particular interest to the topic of 'religion, gender and development' is the paper by Emma Tomalin 2007: Gender Studies approaches to religion and development: literature review (working paper no. 8).

3 Women's rights and fundamentalisms

Gita Sahgal and Nira Yural-Davis (eds) 1992: **Refusing Holy Orders: Women and Fundamentalism in Britain.** **London: Virago.**

This is a landmark text that opened up many of the debates that are now current around issues of women's rights and religious fundamentalisms. The focus is British, but it has a broader relevance to other contexts. A key message of the book is that fundamentalisms are not just found within Islam but have the potential to emerge from within all religious traditions. The chapters deal with a range of religions, including Christianity, Islam and Judaism, and draw attention to the ways in which identity, gender roles, and attitudes towards contraception and work become refocused as issues of control and, at the same time, resistance.

John S. Hawley (ed) 1994: *Fundamentalism and Gender.* **New York; Oxford: Oxford University Press.**

The introduction to this edited volume traces the meaning of the term 'fundamentalism' back to its origins in 19th century North American Protestantism. The book suggests that while there are problems with the cross-cultural use of the term (since it is loaded and increasingly reflects Western negativity towards certain types of Islam) different forms of 'fundamentalism' do share family resemblances, such as conservative attitudes towards gender roles. The volume includes articles on North America, Indian Islam, Hinduism, Japanese new religions and Judaism.

Judy Brink and Joan Mencher (eds) 1997: *Mixed Blessing: Gender and Religious Fundamentalism Cross Culturally.* New York: Routledge.

This collection of papers is concerned with the effects of different expressions of fundamentalism on gender roles in a range of cultural settings. It deals with questions of why some women participate in fundamentalist groups and the ways in which fundamentalisms control women's lives and sexuality. The chapters are grouped in three categories: 'women benefit from fundamentalism'; 'women struggle against fundamentalism's restrictions'; and 'women oppressed by fundamentalism'.

Courtney W. Howland 2001: *Religious Fundamentalisms and the Human Rights of Women.* Basingstoke: Palgrave.

The book explores the problems that religious fundamentalisms in Buddhism, Christianity, Hinduism, Islam and Judaism present to women's rights across the globe. While distinct movements exist within different locations and religions, the book argues that there are commonalities in terms of their negative impact on women's rights, across these different types. It includes articles from both academic and activist authors, and from a range of countries. Several themes emerge from the book. First, fundamentalisms are particularly concerned with controlling women's bodies and sexuality; second, there is a need for non-legal, as well as legal, responses to fundamentalisms; and third 'liberals' in the West, through fear of being labelled as racist and in promotion of multiculturalism, have ended up effectively colluding with fundamentalists in failing to condemn the abuse of women's human rights.

Jane H. Bayes and Nayreheh Tohidi (eds) 2001: *Globalization, Gender, and Religion. The Politics of Women's Rights in Catholic and Muslim Contexts.* Basingstoke: Palgrave.

The impetus behind this edited volume was the United Nations Fourth World Conference on Women held in Beijing in 1995. Both Bayes and Tohidi participated in this event and were struck by the way in which some Catholic and Muslim delegates united against certain aspects of women's rights that involved issues of 'sexuality and sexual orientation, women's control of their bodies (including abortion rights – as well as over questions of equity versus equality and sex versus gender' (p. 1). Before presenting a series of essays that investigate this conservative religious outlook, the editors provide a background chapter. Here they discuss traditional Catholic and Muslim attitudes towards women, the ways in which these traditions have responded to globalization and modernity, and the use of religion and spirituality by women working for social change. The essays that follow reflect on the impact of the Beijing 'Platform for Action' upon the lives of women in eight different countries and the extent to which conservatives in each society seek to limit its implementation. Four deal with Catholicism (United States, Republic of Ireland, Spain, and Latin America) and four with Islam (Turkey, Iran, Bangladesh, and Egypt).

4 Gender, religion and development

Theodora Foster Carroll 1983: *Women, Religion, and Development in the Third World*. **New York; Eastbourne: Praeger.**

This is quite possibly the first text to directly address the topic of women, religion and development. Carroll notes the fact that secularization is not occurring as predicted in the 'Third World' and that this has negative implications for women's development. However, she does not reject religion for this reason, but instead considers that it can be a positive force for change if it undergoes reform.

Kamla Bhasin, Ritu Menon and Nighat Said Khan 1994: *Against All Odds: Essays on Women, Religion and Development from India and Pakistan*. **New Delhi: Kali for Women; Quezon City, Philippines and Santiago: Isis International; Colombo: South Asia Women's Forum.**

This is an early example of a text arguing for the relevance of religion to development. It recognizes religion as both an impediment to women's development as well as something that can be used strategically to further women's empowerment.

Martha Nussbaum 2000: *Women and Human Development: The Capabilities Approach*. **Cambridge: Cambridge University Press**.

In this book Nussbaum applies the capabilities approach to issues around women's development. This is an approach to development 'that focuses on *human capabilities*, that is, what people are actually able to do and to be' (2000: 5). Chapter three focuses specifically on the tension between 'religious free exercise' and 'sex equality'. The idea of 'religious free exercise', to be able to freely choose to be religious or not, is a democratic freedom in many contexts yet at the same time the fact that religious traditions are not equal in their treatment of men and women has implications for women's rights.

Tamsin Bradley 2006. *Challenging the NGOs: Religion, Western Discourses and Indian Women*. **London: I.B. Tauris.**

This book draws on a series of ethnographic case studies that document the experiences of three Rajasthani village women to argue that the interfaces between religion, gender, anthropology and social development are relevant to the work of NGOs. Bradley argues that NGOs should integrate understandings of these relationships into their work in order to increase the efficiency of their activities.

Tamsin Bradley 2010: *Development and the Role of Religion in Gender: Faith Based Organizations and Dialogues in Development.* **London: IB Tauris.**

In this book Bradley argues that it is important to mainstream not only gender analysis but also considerations of religion, within contemporary development theory and practice. This argument is timely and important, and corresponds with recent shifts in both academic research and public policy that recognize the crucial roles that religion plays in developing countries. However, the gender implications of the religion–development nexus have been given less attention and it is this aspect that she brings to the fore.

5 Postcolonial theory and reflections on religion and gender

Uma Narayan 1997: *Dislocating Cultures: Identities, Traditions and Third World Feminism.* **New York and London: Routledge.**

This text is concerned with the ways in which Third World cultures and feminist agendas have been misrepresented by Western feminists and other scholars since colonial times. These misrepresentations, Narayan argues, pose problems for developing respect for difference and cross-cultural understanding. Chapter three, for instance (Cross-Cultural Connections, Border Crossing and 'Death by culture'), asks why it is that domestic violence in the USA is rarely seen as a 'cultural' issue, whereas in India domestic violence is only really considered in terms of 'dowry death' which is depicted in the media and by academics as a matter of culture.

Laura E. Donaldson and Kwok Pui-lan (eds) 2002: *Postcolonialism, Feminism and Religious Discourse.* **New York and London: Routledge.**

This is a significant text that not only brings together issues around feminism and religion, but more importantly locates these within postcolonial contexts and discourses. The postcolonial insights that it brings to the study of gender and religion are relevant for thinking about these topics in the context of development concerns. The essays deal with examples of when religion maintains and shapes colonialist attitudes and where religion has the capacity to challenge and transform these. The essays are from a range of geographical locations and religious traditions.

Ursula King and Tina Beattie 2004: *Gender, Religion and Diversity: Cross-Cultural Perspectives.* **London and New York: Continuum.**

This book contains a combination of more theoretical and 'theological' work and that which is concerned with the wider cultural and contextual implications of religion for gender across traditions and geographical regions. The first section gives an insight into the diversity of theoretical approaches that have been applied to the study of religion and its intersections with questions of gender, culture, ethnicity, plurality, postmodernism and postcoloniality. The second section of the book presents material about the representation of gender in the study of religious texts and historical contexts. The final section is concerned with the application of theoretical approaches to studying religion and gender to actual contexts.

6 Women and religion

There is a large body of literature in this area. Many texts are concerned with the 'theology' behind various interpretations of religious traditions that oppress women as well as those that empower them. There are also texts that link these theologies to particular contexts and socio-political environments. Thus, the degree to which texts in this area are directly related to development issues varies. Below is a small selection of literature that engages with issues around women's rights, politics and social action.

Chien-Yu Julia Huang and Robert P. Weller 1998: Merit and Mothering: Women and Social Welfare in Taiwanese Buddhism. *The Journal of Asian Studies*, 57(2), pp. 379–96.

In this article we learn about the largest social welfare organization in Taiwan – the Tzu Chi Foundation. It was established by a Buddhist nun and largely involves female volunteers. The authors demonstrate that women who volunteer for this movement are shifting their traditional Confucian 'mothering' role in the family to the social sphere through their involvement in Tzu Chi.

Rebecca Foley 2004: Muslim Women's Challenges to Islamic Law: The Case of Malaysia. *International Feminist Journal of Politics*, 6 (1), pp. 53–84.

Sleboda, J. 2001: Islam and women's rights advocacy in Malaysia. *Asian Journal of Women's Studies*, 7(2), pp. 94–136.

Both of these articles are interested in the ways in which some Muslim women in Malaysia are challenging Islamic law through reinterpretations of religious texts. They both illustrate their work with the example of the organization 'Sisters in Islam', a group of feminist Shari'ah lawyers.

Amina Jamal 2005: Feminist 'selves' and feminism's others: feminist representatives of Jamaat-e-Islami women in Pakistan. *Feminist Review*, 81, pp. 52–73.

This article discusses the ways in which Islamic political movements, such as the political party Jamaat-e-Islami, are becoming important sites for women's activism while at the same time seeking to harness that activism for agendas that seem to act against women's autonomy. Jamal argues that understanding the subject-position of Muslim women has meant a conceptual crisis for feminism in Pakistan and that the secular feminist movement has been forced to rethink the boundaries between the religious and the secular.

Tamsin Bradley and Emma Tomalin 2010: The contemporary dowry problematic: exploring the role of the study of religion in bridging the gap between theory and practice. *Religions of South Asia*, 3(2): 251–74.

This article explores the 'contemporary dowry problematic' through a 'study of religions' perspective. The argument made is that, for religious women, challenges to dowry will often be made by them from within their religious tradition. Whilst feminist scholars recognize the role that religion plays in shaping patriarchal practices such as dowry, ignoring the significance of religion in the lives of many women will only serve to marginalize them further from the anti-dowry campaign. This article considers what anti-dowry activists, who are mainly secular, can gain from a more sympathetic view of religion.

Alf Hiltebeital and Kathleen M. Erndl 2000: *Is the Goddess a Feminist? The Politics of South Asian Goddesses*. Sheffield: Sheffield Academic Press.

This book is interested in the politicization of South Asian goddesses. While these figures have become positive resources for branches of the feminist movement in the West, this is problematic and more complex in a South Asian context where they are the product of a patriarchal society, on the one hand, and have been drawn into divisive forms of communal politics, on the other.

Isabel Apawo Phiri and Sarojini Nadar 2006: *African Women, Religion and Health: Essays in Honor of Mercy Amba Ewudziwa Oduyoye (Women from the Margins)*. Maryknoll, New York: Orbis Books.

Mercy Amba Oduyoye, from Ghana, is one of the foremost African feminist theologians and founder of the Circle of Concerned African Women, having also served as the Deputy General Secretary of the World Council of Churches. In addition to establishing her contribution to the field, the focus of the book is on women's health and HIV/AIDS. Another text that deals with similar topics is:

Musa W. Dube and Musimbi Kanyoro (eds) 2004: *Grant Me Justice! HIV/AIDS and Gender Readings of the Bible*. Maryknoll, New York: Orbis Books.

Maria Pilar Aquino 1993: *Our Cry for Life: Feminist Theology from Latin America*. Translated by D. Livingstone. Maryknoll, New York: Orbis Books.

Aquino is one of the most prominent Latin American feminist theologians. In this book she considers that Latin American women's theology should not be seen as something separate from liberation theology, but that the latter has failed to adequately incorporate a feminist vision into its approach.

Milagros Peña 1995: Christian Women in Latin America: Other Voices, Other Visions. *Journal of Feminist Studies in Religion*, **(11)1: pp. 81–94**

This article looks at the emergence of feminist Catholic organizations in Latin America since the 1970s, which challenge the patriarchy of the Catholic Church and its dominance over the lives of women and men. In a more recent book by the same author, *Latina Activists Across Borders: Women's Grassroots Organizing in Mexico and Texas* (Durham, N.C.: Duke University Press 2007) she examines two groups of women activists, drawing attention to the alliances formed with other women's organizations, including Catholic women's groups.

Note

1   http://www.unrisd.org/unrisd/website/projects.nsf/(httpProjectsForPro-grammeArea-en)/3F3D45E0F8567920C12572B9004180C5?OpenDocument

Index

Oxfam GB is a development, relief, and campaigning organization that works with others to find lasting solutions to poverty and suffering around the world. Oxfam GB is a member of Oxfam International. As part of its programme work, Oxfam GB undertakes research and documents its programme and humanitarian experience. This is disseminated through books, journals, policy papers, research reports, and campaign reports which are available for free download at: www.oxfam.org.uk/publications

www.oxfam.org.uk
Email: publish@oxfam.org.uk
Tel: +44 (0) 1865 472482
Oxfam House
John Smith Drive
Cowley
Oxford, OX4 2JY

The chapters in this book are available for download from the Oxfam GB website: www.oxfam.org.uk/publications

The Working in Gender and Development series brings together themed selections of the best articles from the journal *Gender & Development* and other Oxfam publications for development practitioners and policy makers, students and academics. Titles in the series present the theory and practice of gender-oriented development in a way that records experience, describes good practice, and shares information about resources. Books in the series will contribute to and review current thinking on the gender dimensions of particular development and relief issues.

Other titles in the series include:
Gender-Based Violence
HIV and AIDS
Climate Change and Gender Justice
Gender and the Economic Crisis